The Scituate Historical Society exists for the purpose of educating all who seek knowledge of the history of the town and people of Scituate and those municipalities that were anciently a part of the town, through the publication of printed material, public lectures, thoroughly descriptive tours of Scituate's historic sites, and the continued growth of a volunteer-staffed and free-to-the-public historical and genealogical library, with a strong interest in instilling a sense of stewardship of the town's history in schoolchildren. As stewards of the town's most precious historic landmarks, the Society constantly searches for new, innovative, and effective means of raising funds for the continuing preservation efforts at each of the nine sites with which it is associated, with particular emphasis placed on the restoration of the Stockbridge Gristmill, the completion of the George W. Perry Post No. 31, Grand Army Hall Restoration Project, and the overall future financial stability of the organization. The Society acts as a leader and partner in the historic preservation field through collaborative efforts with local, state, national, and international historical, fraternal, municipal, and educational organizations. The Society also reaches out to the people of the community and region for ideas and input, and works with the local chamber of commerce and regional and state tourism councils to increase tourism to the South Shore of Boston, promoting and celebrating the cultural diversity of Scituate and Plymouth County, Massachusetts.

Beauty, Strength, Speed:

Celebrating 100 Years of Thomas W. Lawson's Dreamwold

*By Carol Miles and
John J. Galluzzo*

Copyright © 2002 by the Scituate Historical Society

All rights reserved, including the right to reproduce this work in any form whatsoever without permission in writing from the publisher, except for brief passages in connection with a review. For information, write:

The Donning Company Publishers
184 Business Park Drive, Suite 206
Virginia Beach, VA 23462

Steve Mull, General Manager
Mary Taylor, Project Director
Susan Adams, Project Research Coordinator
Dawn V. Kofroth, Assistant General Manager
Sally Clarke Davis, Editor
Bridget Belmont, Graphic Designer
John Harrell, Imaging Artist
Scott Rule, Director of Marketing

Library of Congress Cataloging-in-Publication Data
Miles, Carol, 1932–
   Beauty, strength, speed : celebrating 100 years of Thomas W. Lawson's Dreamwold / by Carol Miles and John J. Galluzzo.
     p. cm.
   Includes bibliographical references (p.).
   ISBN 1-57864-171-3 (soft cover)
   1. Lawson, Thomas William, 1857–1925. 2. Businessmen—Biography. 3. Lawson, Thomas William, 1857–1925—Homes and haunts—Massachusetts—Scituate. I. Galluzzo, John. II. Title.

HG172. L39 M55 2002
974.4'82—dc21

2002025711

Printed in the United States of America

THE
DONNING COMPANY
PUBLISHERS

Table of Contents

Preface — *6*

Introduction — *7*

Chapter One. An Old Town by the Sea: Scituate in 1900 — *12*

Chapter Two. With Princely Munificence: The Building of Dreamwold Farm — *26*

Chapter Three. A Comfortable Country Home: The Dreamwold Farmhouse — *42*

Chapter Four. For the Benefit of Half the County: Lawson Tower — *52*

Chapter Five. A More Simple and Lovable Crudity: Tom Lawson Speaks His Mind — *64*

Chapter Six. An Emblem of Victory Birthed From Suffering: The Story of Lawson Common — *78*

Chapter Seven. Larger Than Life — *98*

Postscript — *113*

Select Bibliography — *124*

About the Authors — *126*

Acknowledgments — *127*

Preface

There may never be a complete biography of Thomas W. Lawson, for there are simply more stories, tales, legends, and anecdotes about him than any one person, or in this case, any one historical society, can collect. You may not find your favorite Lawson story in this book. That's probably because we haven't heard it yet.

Instead of taking on the enormous task of encapsulating Lawson's entire life in these pages, we have chosen to focus on his Scituate years, 1900–25, and what has become of his extensive property holdings in the ensuing three quarters of a century since his passing. Our introduction will settle you, the reader, in time, and our first chapter will give you a sense of place; from that point on, we let the magic of Thomas W. Lawson carry you forward.

Lawson's story is a classic American "rags to riches" tale. He began his working life shoveling gold coins into a sack in a Boston bank. His Wall Street wizardry with both Standard Oil and his own copper concerns amassed him an enormous fortune by 1900. His brash outspokenness cost him that fortune just two decades later. In the meantime he lived his life the way he dreamed it would be as a boy, marrying the only love of his life, Jeannie Augusta Goodwillie, and devoting his every moment to her happiness. When she died in 1906 at forty-eight years old, his life lost much of its meaning. From that point he focused his attention on the lives of his six children, Arnold, Gladys, Marion, Dorothy, Douglas, and Jean. Although he reveled in the various passions of his life, including fine art, fine dogs, and fine horses, nothing rivaled his pursuit of the uninterrupted happiness of his family.

One hundred years has passed since the chimes of Lawson Tower first rang out across the South Shore of Massachusetts. One hundred years has passed since the launch of the world's only seven-masted steel schooner, the ship that bore Lawson's name. One hundred years has passed since Tom Lawson first opened his Dreamwold gates to visitors. This book is long overdue.

Introduction

At the turn of the twentieth century, Americans reveled in the fact that life had never at any other point in history moved at such an excitingly accelerated pace. Technological innovations seemed to appear on a daily basis. New communication devices such as the telegraph and the telephone had corrupted all concepts of distance and time. To get a message to Aunt Martha in Detroit took a week or two by mail in the past; in 1900, a phone call made the connection instantly.

In effect, according to Charles Morris' *Famous Men and Great Events of the Nineteenth Century*, Elisha Gray had even invented the world's first fax machine in the 1800s. "Extraordinary progress has been made in systems of telegraphy, some of the new inventions being capable of remarkable feats in the rapid sending of messages, while it is possible now to transmit pictures as well as words over the telegraphic wire."

The industrial revolution that dominated the nineteenth century created the concept of the vacation by causing a rift in the American economic class structure. Business owners allowed their empires to run themselves in summer as they made their retreats for rest and relaxation along the shoreline, or in the mountains. No longer tied to the soil and farming, they abandoned the Puritan work ethic that had formed the American way of life since the 1600s for clambakes, band concerts, parades, yacht races, and cool starlit evenings on the porch. For day trips, they clamored aboard their automobiles, or horseless carriages; for extended trips, they boarded trains to see places of which their parents and grandparents had only read or fantasized.

So it should come as no surprise that the citizenry of the United States looked to the future with a tremendous amount of hope in 1900, and with an eye focused on the scientists, engineers, and inventors of the world. John Elfreth Watkins, Jr., shared his predictions for the twentieth century with the readers of the December 1900 *Ladies' Home Journal* through his article: "What May Happen in the Next Hundred Years."

"Grand opera will be telephoned to private homes, and will sound as harmonious as though enjoyed from a theatre box," he states, referring to the impending invention of the radio. "Automobiles will have been substituted for every horse vehicle now known. There will be, as already exists today, automobile hearses, automobile police patrols, automobile ambulances, automobile street sweepers. The horse in harness will be as scarce, if, indeed, not even scarcer, than the yoked ox is today.

"There will be air-ships," he continues. "They will be maintained as deadly war vessels by all military nations. Some will transport men and goods. Others will be used by scientists making observations at great heights above the earth.

"Photographs will be telegraphed from any distance. If there be a battle in China a hundred years hence snapshots of its most striking events will be published in the newspapers an hour later. Photographs will reproduce all of Nature's colors.

"A husband in the middle of the Atlantic will be able to converse with his wife sitting in her boudoir in Chicago. We will be able to telephone to China quite readily as we now talk from New York to Brooklyn. By an automatic signal they will connect with any circuit in their locality without the intervention of a 'hello girl.'

"Hot or cold air will be turned on from spigots to regulate the temperature of a house as we now turn on hot or cold water from spigots to regulate the temperature of the bath. . . . Rising early to build the furnace fire will be a task of the olden times."

Of course, not all of Watkins' predictions could come true. "There will be no C, X, or Q in our every-day alphabet. They will be abandoned because unnecessary. Spelling by sound will have been adopted, first by the newspapers. Everybody will walk ten miles. Gymnastics will begin in the nursery, where toys and games will be designed to strengthen the muscles . . . A man or woman unable to walk ten miles at a stretch will be regarded as a weakling. A university education will be free to every man and woman."

Watkins also fell prey to the notion that pneumatic tubes would be the cure-all invention of the century. "Ready-cooked meals will be bought from establishments similar to our bakeries of to-day . . . Food will be served hot or cold to private houses in pneumatic tubes or automobile wagons. The meal being over, the dishes used will be packed and returned to the cooking establishments where they will be washed. Such wholesale cookery will be done in electric laboratories rather than in kitchens. These laboratories will be equipped with electric stoves, and all sorts of electric devices, such as coffee-grinders, egg-beaters, stirrers, shakers, parers, meat-choppers, meat-saws, potato-mashers, lemon-squeezers, dish-washers, dish-dryers and the like. All such utensils will be washed in chemicals fatal to disease microbes. Having one's own cook and purchasing one's own food will be an extravagance."

John Douglas King, chief inspector of the New York Post Office in 1900, believed that pneumatic tubes would revolutionize our mail system. "He predicts that letter postage will be reduced to one cent per half ounce, that letters will be shot directly from the post office to business houses, hotels, etc., by the pneumatic tube system." (Morris, p. 659.)

The Victorians held firm beliefs that the power of the mind would someday be fully realized and put to use in a plethora of advantageous ways. A Professor Quackenbos of Columbia University promoted hypnotic suggestion as a future medicinal aid. "I believe that as an agent of physical cure it will shortly come to be universally employed by trained nurses to carry their patients through the crises of disease. It will be used by physicians for intra-uterine inspiration, the character of the forming child will be determined by ante-natal suggestion, and this method of improving ethically and intellectually a coming generation will be practiced on so large and broad a scale that society will feel the uplift." (Morris, pp. 662–3.)

One man, Richard le Galliene, predicted that authors would someday shake off the shackles of the typewriter and the pen and directly mind-link with their readers. "It seems not unlikely that with the advance of science some more direct medium between the mind of the writer and the mind of the reader may be invented by some Edison of the future, some marvelously delicate instrument, not impossible to imagine, by which, on the one hand, the writer could record his thought without the medium of words at all, and by which, on the other, the reader could receive them equally without words or print." (Morris, p. 661.)

Cynics, of course, existed. Russian writer Eugene Markov saw the formation of dangerous trends in the latter half of the nineteenth century, the continuation of which could perceivably cause the downfall of society. "One fears for the future of mankind. The most ominous sign is not the fact that the cook, servant-girl, and lackey want the same pleasures which not long ago were the monopoly of the rich alone; but the fact that all, all without exception, rich and idle as well as poor and industrious, seek and demand daily amusements, gaiety, excitement and keen impressions – demand it all as something without which life is impossible, which may not be denied them."

The editors of the *New York World* figured that if the twentieth century would bring an end to the civilized world, they would be the first to predict its causes by polling a wide assortment of eminent gentlemen. Mark Sullivan's *Our Times* collected the prognostications. Arthur Conan Doyle, the literary genius behind Sherlock Holmes, felt anxiety about the growing tendency towards "an ill-balanced, excitable, and sensation-mongering press." President Hadley of Yale feared "legislation based on the self-interest of individuals, or classes, instead of on public sentiment and public spirit." Dean Farrar declared the "dominance of drink" as our greatest potential social evil. The Bishop of Gloucester decried "self-advertising vanity," while the Archbishop of Canterbury answered the question about what would bring about the downfall of society with a simple, honest, "I have not the slightest idea." (Mark Sullivan, *Our Times,* Vol. 1, p. 372).

With innovations coming by land, air and sea, the industrial revolution's assault on nineteenth century America continued unabated into the twentieth. With eyes wide open, the people of Scituate, Massachusetts rang in the New Year of 1900 as their ancestors had for more than two and a half centuries, completely and innocently unaware of the impending arrival of a man who would change the town's history forever.

Chapter One:
An Old Town by the Sea: Scituate in 1900

There could be no doubting the predominant ethnic make-up of the little town of Scituate, Massachusetts, at the beginning of the twentieth century. The Irish came to town in great numbers on the heels of Boston fisherman Daniel Ward, upon his 1848 discovery that carrageenan, or Irish moss, grew on the underwater rocks off Scituate's shore. The Irish, who brought Catholicism to town with them, harvested the moss, dried it, and shipped it off to be used as a lightening agent in beer and a thickening agent in cough syrup, among other products, starting an industry that lasted for a century and a half in Scituate. On July 12, 1901, a scribe working for the Vining syndicate of South Shore newspapers under the nom de plume "The Saunterer," reported that during one of his summer visits to Scituate the Irish influence could not be denied. "One thing that impressed itself very forcibly upon the mind of The Saunterer was the regularity with which he met red-haired girls. Why there should be more at Scituate harbor than at other places he cannot tell. It may be that the bright sunbeams nestled in their tresses so much that some of their radiance was caught and reflected there. At any rate, red seems to be the prevailing color in hair."

Like most of the residents of the South Shore, Irish mossers were rebuilding their businesses in 1900. The most destructive storm of the previous century had arrived just in time to be considered a nineteenth-century gale, on November 26, 1898. Normally laid out on the beach to dry during the day, part of a ten-to-fourteen-day drying cycle, Irish moss was susceptible to a gelatin breakdown when coming in contact with fresh water. Each night the mossers, their wives, and children collected the moss in barrels and covered it with heavy canvas. The Portland Gale destroyed an estimated one thousand barrels of the product, taking money directly from the pockets of hardworking families who were waiting through the winter for buyers at good prices. Although moss grew (and still grows) abundantly off Scituate, its growth was triggered by warm temperatures. Scituate's mossers would not be able to scrape the rocks again until May or June.

Once the home to sea captains as far as the eye could see, Scituate Harbor and the banks of the North River had seen the construction of 1,025 sailing ships between 1690 and 1870. Virgin timber, access to the sea, and the presence of bog iron ore made the North River an ideal location for early shipwrights. Some of the country's proudest vessels

In 1900, both visitors to Scituate and its own citizenry, like John Prouty and friends, came to see the potential for rest and relaxation along the town's shoreline. (Photo by Frederick Damon)

had been kedged from upriver to the sea, including *Columbia*, the first vessel to circumnavigate the globe under the American flag, and for which the Columbia River in the Pacific Northwest is named, and *Beaver*, remembered for its role in the Boston Tea Party. By the 1850s shipbuilders complained of needing better access to the ocean. At that time river pilots steered their ships within feet of the Atlantic at a barrier beach between Third and Fourth Cliffs, only to turn to the south for another two miles before reaching the mouth of the river.

Frustrated about the future of the industry on the river, the locals petitioned the federal government to direct the Army Corps of Engineers to cut a canal between the cliffs. The government countered by proposing a canal from the North River to Scituate Harbor, to reinvigorate the flow of water into the river. Neither eventuality took place and, in 1870, the *Helen M. Foster*, the last vessel of any size to be built on the North River, slid away to sea. On November 26, 1898, Mother Nature did what the federal government would not, blasting away the barrier beach between the cliffs during the Portland Gale. She was thirty years too late. By 1901, the sounds of hammers, saws, and adzes could only be heard in echoes, as the North River had become a ghost town. "The Harbor is unique in its way," wrote The Saunterer, "with just enough of the old salt flavor to remind one

While Scituate Harbor boomed, life continued at a comfortable pace on Gannett Road in North Scituate. (Scituate Historical Society collection)

Turn-of-the-century Scituate still afforded plenty of forest, marsh, and meadowlands for a good day's hunting. (Photo by Genovese Greeley)

that it was in days gone by somewhat of a seaport town. In the past it was quite a port for fishermen, but like Hingham, Cohasset and other towns along the coast, its glory in that line has departed."

Nevertheless, Scituate began to feel a bit of a boom in 1900. Somewhat geographically secluded, in 1667 its early political leaders had passed a law to punish those folks who extended a hand in friendship to weary travelers: "If any person shall entertayn any stranger, after being admonished by a committee chosen for such purpose, he shall forfeit and pay 10s. for each week." Ironically, with the major industry of shipbuilding gone, Scituate would reinvent itself as a seasonal resort town, building hotels to entice boarders to come and enjoy the sights, sounds, and smells of the sea.

The Saunterer felt that Scituate could thrive as a seasonal destination. "At the present time it is rapidly coming into prominence as a summer resort, its many advantages in the way of pleasant scenery, fine ocean views and invigorating sea breezes rendering it a very desirable place for summer rest and recreation. The Sand Hills, the cliffs and the many beaches within easy reach add to the attractiveness of the locality. All that is needed to make this one of the most popular places of resort upon the South Shore is a line of electrics connecting it with the outside world."

Another anonymous writer for the Vining syndicate, The Middle Street Man, foresaw a magnificent future for the townsfolk, if they could but leap one hurdle. "The only thing that stands in the way of Scituate's progress and prosperity is a sentiment of conservatism, or rather old-fogeyism, which prevents some of the business men from seeing anything larger in the way of money than the quarter which they hear jingling amongst the keys in their pockets."

One progressive businessman in

The homestead made famous by Samuel Woodworth's poem "The Old Oaken Bucket" by 1900 had become a major tourist destination for literarily inspired travelers. (Scituate Historical Society collection)

particular, George F. Welch, drove the upsurge in activity. "In fact," wrote The Saunterer, "he appears to be the real thing at The Harbor, and everybody said he was the man to whom they all looked for inspiration and advice. His extensive business interests are of great importance to the town and his store, storehouses and wharf appear to be the busiest places there. Mr. Welch is very much in evidence in all the country round; his name is heard and seen everywhere."

Scituate Light editor Floretta Vining, visited Scituate from Hull in November 1900. Recording her thoughts for an editorial entitled "An Afternoon in Scituate," she also sang Welch's praises. "All was bustle. The first object that met our view was the establishment of George F. Welch, as fine a store as I ever saw in the country, with a stock unequalled [sic] in a town so far from Boston, and things up to date. I was simply amazed. The paint stock alone filled one side of the building. Handsome furniture, robes of the best, every kind of gardening tools, kitchen and dining room ware of the best quality." Across the street, merchant Charles Frye had taken over the Payley Allen store, a longstanding landmark for the locals. "It would delight anyone to see the stock he keeps. A fine stocked gro-

Old Scituate Lighthouse had lost its lantern room, but not its charm by 1900. (Scituate Historical Society collection)

Beauty, Strength, Speed: Celebrating 100 Years of Thomas W. Lawson's Dreamwold

The fun at Scituate suited all generations. (Photo by Frederick Damon)

Otis Barker turned the stranded Boston pilot boat **Columbia** *into a popular museum shortly after it came aground in 1898. (Photo by Frederick Damon)*

cery, dry goods, wall papers, all kinds of boots and shoes and here you get everything in the crockery line—blue and green plates, large and handsome pitchers with Scituate Light and the Old Oaken Bucket on them. One could not go anywhere and find better souvenir gifts."

Away from the fast pace of The Harbor, life in Scituate's other villages moved at varying speeds, a little quicker in North Scituate, Minot, Scituate Center, the Sand Hills, and the now-disjointed Humarock peninsula than at Greenbush or in the West End. Visitors seeing Scituate for the first time came for the sailing, fishing, and clean ocean air, but also to spy Old Scituate Light on Cedar Point, doused in 1860, made famous by the heroism of Abigail and Rebecca Bates during the War of 1812, and the Old Oaken Bucket Homestead. Poet Samuel Woodworth's lament for his childhood days in Scituate had drawn international attention to the old New England town in 1842. A half century later, the "deep-tangled wildwood," "wide-spreading pond and the mill that stood by it," and even "the rude bucket that hung in the well," remained as rustically picturesque as they had been during Woodworth's youth.

Taking the train to and from The Harbor, the changeable natural beauty of Scituate manifested itself to travelers. "Riding through the town on the line of the railroad," wrote the Middle Street Man, "one would get the impression that the town was mostly composed of rocks, with a large amount of scrub oak forest, interspersed here and there with a few fertile acres and an occasional farm house, while now and then a church spire in the distance, with a school house close by, shows that the church and school go side by side.

"But the view obtained from a car window can give one but a very erroneous impression of the beauties of Scituate scenery. Inland there are many large and attractive farm houses, surrounded by a large acreage of productive land, with attractive surroundings, while its seacoast has features of beauty possessed by no other resort from Quincy to Plymouth."

In these quieter sections, the people of Scituate went about their daily lives as their ancestors had before them. Just outside the harbor, First and Second Cliffs remained largely unbuilt upon, havens for artists, actors, and writers seeking inspiration. "Art hath its votaries in Scituate," wrote one visitor, writing for *New England Magazine*. "Artists . . . are never in want of fresh material in the ever-varying aspects of earth, sea and sky: the whitening lines of surf roaring along the cliffs; the mile of inturned stone ridge below Third Cliff, often half-matted over with the tide-wash of curious seaweed and Irish moss, and commanding the double prospect of inrolling Atlantic to the east and broad marshes to the west, threaded by silvery channels, dotted with gunners' huts, and enlivened by the flight of sea fowl overhead; or the thick hedges, wild vines of grape, bushes of elderberry, sumach, teeming orchards and stately elms of the inland roadways; or, seen from a cliff road, the harvest moon, emerging in tranquil majesty from the black watery waste and transfiguring it with a glory not of earth."

At Greenbush in 1900, the Clapp family shut down their gristmill after approximately two hundred and fifty years of continuous use, stretching back to the 1640s through several owners, finding the process of grinding corn with a water-driven mill to finally be economically outdated. At Scituate Center, the dwindling ranks of the George W. Perry Post, Grand Army of the Republic, continued to meet each Memorial Day at their hall on Country Way to pay tribute to their fallen comrades, each year a few more flowers being laid at fresh grave sites, each spring fewer blue uniforms being present. Uncle John Brown,

Beauty, Strength, Speed: Celebrating 100 Years of Thomas W. Lawson's Dreamwold

A close-knit and quiet community in 1900, Scituate was about to change in ways of which its inhabitants had never dreamed. (Photo by Lester Hobson)

the oldest man in Scituate, who had voted for twenty of the first twenty-four presidents, could be seen walking each Sunday from the West End to The Harbor, to visit friends and pass the collection plate at church.

His walk took him past the low rolling hills of Egypt, yet another of the villages of Scituate, northwest of The Harbor, mostly barren, and heavily covered with rocks and thick undergrowth at the turn of the twentieth century. *Harper's New Monthly Magazine* reported in 1878 that the section had derived its odd name "from the circumstance that in a time of drought old Squire Pierce had prudently accumulated a store of grain, and neighbors whose supply became exhausted resorted to him for more. He hailed them with, 'Well, boys, so you've come down to Egypt to buy corn!'" According to Scituate historian Charles Wellington Furlong, though, "this seems to be an exploded tradition. Others say this part of Scituate got its name because Egypt in the Bible means 'to get corn,' and that the old sea captains and others used to speak of going to that part of Scituate as 'down to get corn.' But when they used that phrase, they meant corn in its most liquid and vital extract.

"However, others dispute this and say that the old sea captains were God fearing people, which was true without doubt. Some say, that anyway when they did drink in these parts that Old John Barleycorn was in the discard and they drank rum. However, there was the old inn in Egypt on the corner of Captain Pierce Road and Country Way, and undoubtedly many who frequented it, went for other purposes than a glass of sweet cider."

Scituate, especially sleepy and sylvan Egypt, forever lost its low profile with the world in the opening years of the twentieth century. As stated by writer Hayes Robbins in an article entitled "An Old Town by the Sea" in *New England Magazine*, the upcoming changes would not be "overdone to the point of destroying Scituate's rural charm and the true salt flavor of the sea coast," yet rather left the town "somewhat modified, indeed, but unspoiled by gimcrack amusements and huge disfigurements of nature."

Instead, for the third time in less than one hundred years, the world's eyes would turn to Scituate, not to view its heroism in the face of attacking navies, or to seek the poetry inspiring vagaries of its varied landscape, but instead to watch the construction of one of the most storied farm estates in American history. Floretta Vining's words on the coming of Dreamwold to Scituate spoke volumes in November 1900: "I hear Tom Lawson has bought fifty acres and intends to improve it very much. What a future this town has in store for it."

Chapter Two
With Princely Munificence: The Building of Dreamwold Farm

For every documented, factual story about the life of Thomas W. Lawson, there seems to be a perfectly counterbalanced apocryphal tale. To this day, Scituate historians have no proof as to which side of the fence the following story falls.

They do know that Lawson had rented a summer home in Cohasset, the estate of Dr. John Bryant, in 1901, but how he came to choose Scituate for his stock farm is unknown. Local legend says that he and his wife Jeannie were out for a drive in a carriage one warm day in Scituate when they came to a halt in the vicinity of Egypt. Mrs. Lawson, admiring the view and the landscape, commented that the spot where they stood would be a wonderful place for a home. Somehow, through the tangled briars and unending acres of rocks, she envisioned a potential paradise. Tom Lawson, the dream maker, did not let the words go unnoticed.

The local South Shore newspapers got wind of every bit of gossip at the turn of the century, more often than not acting simply as social registers for the seaside resort towns between Hingham and Duxbury. A man with the reputation of Thomas W. Lawson would find it hard to keep his business to himself. The February 1, 1901 edition of the *Scituate Light* reported that a local contractor, Arthur Mulvey, had been in discussions with Lawson and had landed the first contract for grading and constructing roads and track on a new estate, to be built on the site of Mrs. Lawson's vision. "The whole outlay will be something in excess of $100,000, and it is quite a feather in the cap of Mr. Mulvey to be able to land such a big contract, against the competition of some of the largest construction firms in the country. Mr. Mulvey, though a young man, is certainly a live one."

As his plans for Dreamwold, as he would call his estate, began to take shape, Lawson and his family spent their time in neighboring Cohasset. Unable to buy the Bryant

house overlooking the Cohasset Yacht Club, he chose to make improvements around it instead, building a bungalow and purchasing for ten times its value and then demolishing a small home that blocked a view that he wanted. His daughters soon made their impression on the South Shore, described on July 12 as "easily the prettiest girls at Cohasset" that summer season. "Miss Gladys Lawson . . . is T.W. Lawson's eldest daughter, and a 'stunning' girl. She likes to ride, drive, play golf, tennis, row a boat or paddle a canoe, and she loves the water. She has four blue ribbon horses and can drive them cleverly."

By June, the magnitude of Lawson's project started to drop the jaws of the local populace in amazement, as reported in the *Scituate Light* on the eighth. "The attention of passengers on the Plymouth division trains is daily attracted to a gang of several hundred workmen on a piece of recently cleared land just below Scituate and the trainmen are bombarded with questions every time they pass.

"It is the beginning of another of Thomas W. Lawson's great enterprises, and the

Thomas W. Lawson's dream estate would never have come to be without the work of approximately one thousand laborers, who started the building process by removing acre after acre of rocks. (Photo by T. E. Marr)

Dreamwold featured miles of sturdy, well-built roads. (Photo by T. E. Marr)

once desolate and unattractive brushwood patch will soon be the home of blooded horses and one of the great points of interest on the shore. A race track and stables are being constructed. The foundations of the stables, already laid, give an idea of the mammoth proportions of the buildings. The main stable for the blooded racing and fancy stock is 800 feet in length, the farm stable and barn will be 200 feet long and the cow barn is 175 feet. They are all in a straight line.

"Mr. Lawson is establishing a great stock farm on the land and there will be a large farm house with all the modern conveniences, surrounded by beautiful lawns and throughout the grounds the finest macadam driveways will be laid. The farm will be enclosed by six miles of fencing.

"A mile track is being constructed on the most approved scientific plan and is calculated to be very fast. The New York, New Haven and Hartford will run a spur into the premises."

That same week Lawson rented a cottage at Point Allerton in Hull to spend "such leisure time as is left him from the numerous other directions in which his energies are turned."

At the height of his fortune, Lawson's holdings totaled sixty million dollars, gath-

Beauty, Strength, Speed: Celebrating 100 Years of Thomas W. Lawson's Dreamwold

Left: The impressive riding academy building could be dressed for parties, or used for indoor exercise of the blooded stock during bad weather. (Photo by T. E. Marr) Below: A horse and driver emerge from the most magnificent building on the estate, the eight-hundred-foot-long racing stable. (Photo by T. E. Marr)

With Princely Munificence: The Building of Dreamwold Farm

Right: Lawson believed that if his stallions could see each other in their stalls, they would become violent. Therefore, he built them a horseshoe-shaped stable. (Photo by T. E. Marr) Below: Telephones, as seen on the right here in the stallion stable, connected all of the buildings on the estate. (Photo by T. E. Marr)

ered mostly by cornering the copper market. Carried forward to 2002, he would have been worth approximately 1.2 billion dollars. The South Shore had never seen such wealth.

The job of building Dreamwold fell to the nearly one thousand workmen he hired for the purpose, instructed that "Everything must be heavy, strong, simple and quiet; if four by six will do, make it six by eight." Beginning in that winter of 1900–01, they set out to clear the land. As stated by writer E. C. Lincoln in *The National Sportsman* in September, 1902, Lawson "took a tremendous tract of this unhappy looking land and literally made it over to his purpose. The rocks and stones were torn from their places and made to serve him in his roadways, drives and pathways; to enrich the soil, immense quantities of loam were hauled to the farm and distributed as needed." Locals were told that if they chopped down the trees on any given acre of his land, they could take it home for firewood. By summer, buildings began to rise. As the work continued, Lawson celebrated the Fourth of July with his family in Cohasset, financing the greatest display of fireworks that community had ever seen. In November, he retreated to his permanent residence at Charlesgate East in Boston, keeping an eye on the estate's progress at all times. In December, the first two carloads of what would be one of the world's most

Harnessed for show, Dainty Dappho and Ruritania pull a light carriage. (Photo by T. E. Marr)

magnificent collections of horses arrived at Egypt.

The *Scituate Light* carried the news of the estate week by week. By January 10, the steel riding academy was nearly completed; by January 17, a large number of valuable hens had been received; by January 24, trees had been removed from a nursery in Cohasset to be planted at Dreamwold, the same week that Lawson contracted thirteen new buildings for the estate. In early February, as another carload of horses arrived (and he sent two to the Barnum and Bailey circus), he arranged for his son Arnold and daughters Gladys and Marion to visit Cairo. There they would meet Lionel Lawson, the nephew of Sir Wilfred Lawson of England and one of the under secretaries of the viceroy of India, before heading to India and then to England to attend the coronation of King Edward VII.

By March of 1902, the *Cohasset Sentinel* hinted that Lawson's interests may finally have lured his thoughts away from that town altogether. "Mr. Thomas W. Lawson doesn't know where he belongs. He longs for Cohasset and yet his buildings are in Scituate, and his railroad station in Egypt." Through the spring of 1902, he continued purchasing land around his original purchases, expanding his estate. More and more local workmen were hired for varied tasks, prompting the editor of the *Scituate Light* to remark, "Mr. Thomas W. Lawson is doing the best he knows how. He is buying land at big prices, and, with princely munificence, giving the buildings thereon to their former owners. He is employing hundreds of men at good wages and making a paradise of the

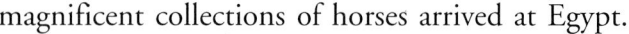

The most modern convenience, electricity, could still be dressed to look rustic, as on the numerous light poles erected throughout the estate at two-hundred-foot intervals. (Photo by T. E. Marr)

Beauty, Strength, Speed: Celebrating 100 Years of Thomas W. Lawson's Dreamwold

old useless bush pastures. He took that hideous structure, the water company's standpipe, and at an enormous expense made it an ornament to the country side. He is distributing his millions sensibly."

Although the estate had not nearly been completed, Lawson opened the grounds to the public on Patriots Day in April 1902, to coincide with the Plymouth County Convention of the Grand Army of the Republic. What the visitors saw that day, as described by Lincoln, left them in awe. "After alighting from the train at Egypt . . . the lodge and the magnificent gate, near the great racing stable, first greets the eye, a monument in itself, a fitting herald of the glories within. Inside, but a short distance away, is the stable, a tremendous structure, 800 feet long, and not far from that is the riding academy and the stable for short tailed horses." The 800-foot racing stable, perhaps the grandest structure of them all, had been completed in seventy-two working days, "of mill construction in five-foot bays . . . divided into sections by automatic fire-proof curtains and the lofts by self-closing fire doors."

A special edition of *The Architectural Review* detailed the estates buildings. All of

Below: Each building at Dreamwold displayed its own distinctive, hand-forged, wrought iron sign. (Photo by T. E. Marr)
Left: The Dreamwold blacksmith shop had room for the shoeing of eight horses at once, which must have come in handy on an estate with more than three hundred of the animals at one time. (Photo by T. E. Marr)

The kennel building, today a private home, provided private romping yards for some of Lawson's favorite pets. (Photo by T. E. Marr)

the stables on the property—foaling, farm horse, carriage horse, and three broodmares—had been designed with the comfort of their inhabitants in mind. "Each horse in his stall can look toward the south and get the southerly breezes, while the partitions of his box stall and the thickness of the outer wall protect him from the wintry winds off the ocean." Only the stallion stable varied from this particular linear arrangement, built in the shape of a horseshoe instead, as Lawson feared that if they had been able to see one another, the fierce and competitive nature of his stallions would cause their tempers to flare. Spruce floors, replaced every six to twelve months, provided a healthier alternative to clay, dirt, or brick. Vents carried fresh air into the individual stalls during the winter, with hay manually fed to each feeding station by pitchfork.

Stable hands lived on the second and third floors above the stables, the racing stable coming complete with a "dining room sixty feet long, a kitchen, pantries, an elevator, store rooms, and a huge refrigerator." The second story also contained "recreation rooms, a library and the general bath rooms."

The riding academy, completed in fifty-six days, held an oval ring one hundred and eight feet by one hundred and seventy feet, affording "exercise room for rainy days and in cold weather, on a tan bark floor," overlooked by a gallery and lit by four Nernst lamps. Eventually, more than three hundred horses would call Dreamwold home. "Not far from the racing stable," continues Lincoln, "in a space of ground lower than the surrounding country and forming in itself a picturesque valley in this place of enchantment, is one of the principal show places of the estate, the half mile race track. In the centre is the polo field surrounded by an exercise track for horses, and outside of that enclosing the whole is the superb oval upon which to speed the famous racers of the magnificent stud owned by Mr. Lawson. Overlooking the whole is an artistic creation in the form of a judge's stand, from which all parts of the enclosure can readily be observed." The Dreamwold blacksmith shop was large enough to shoe eight horses at one time.

Each of the buildings on the estate were connected by telephones, still more than a convenience for any household in 1902. Conduit pipe running underground carried electricity throughout the estate, to the buildings and to the rustic lamps that lined its roads every two hundred feet, while an alarm system warned the estate's firemen, who had their own engine, hook and ladder, and hose trucks, in times of emergency. High pressure water ran to each building, and sewage could be conveyed by pipe to Dreamwold's own sewage station.

The entire estate carried a single Dutch-colonial architectural theme, with gambrel-style roofs, chosen by Lawson personally. "At every point the effect is perfect harmony, not one discordant note, quiet, subdued, perfect. Buildings of weatherbeaten grey, similar yet not one like another, each a compliment and artistic offset to its neighbor, and the whole blended into a complete and perfect picture that brings rapture to the soul of an artist." Each building also displayed its own hand-forged and unique wrought-iron sign, depicting an image of what kind of animal could be found

Of all the dogs in the world, Thomas Lawson loved English bulls, like Glen Monarch, the best. (Photo by T. E. Marr)

beyond the doors.

Lawson's love of dogs, especially English bulls, drove the construction of a 225-foot kennel building. Each kennel opened to a yard, stated *The Architectural Review*. "The yards are bounded by galvanized iron posts set in concrete with cypress boards going six inches below the surface and three feet above. Above the boarding is a five-foot wire fence for the bull dogs and a three-foot wire fence for the spaniels. Shelters are provided in each yard and the yards are so arranged that the dogs can be either confined in the smaller runs or turned into the long runs for exercise." Lawson owned more than 150 dogs in approximately six breeds, more than one hundred of them English bulls.

His cow barn, not yet inhabited by Patriots Day, 1902, reversed the construction of the horse barns. The cows, when they arrived, faced north instead of south. "This leaves the gutters toward the south where they receive sunlight, a great factor in keeping this portion of the stable dry and sweet." Two cows stood in each stall, sharing two mangers and one water trough. The passageway through the stable was wide enough for a wagon to pass through, easing the feeding process. A silo stood at either end.

The poultry, bantam, duck, and pigeon—or more likely dove—houses provided shelter for Lawson's feathered friends, while a nearby Dutch-style windmill

As can be seen to the left, Lawson's cow barn had halls wide enough to allow a wagon to pass through to deliver fresh hay. (Photo by T. E. Marr)

ground ensilage for feed. Numerous cottages throughout the estate housed the managers of the various departments of the farm. Dreamwold Hall itself looked like three buildings in one.

The 1902 Patriots Day crowd had just caught the very beginning of the magic of Dreamwold. Five miles of Kentucky fence, much of which can still be seen along Branch Street today, was yet to be built. In late April, workmen planted hundreds of rose bushes, and in May, thousands more shrubs went into the ground. On Monday, May 19, 1902, the Lawson Flyer went into commission, thenceforth whisking Lawson directly from his estate to Boston in under forty minutes.

On May 30, Lawson took one final large step toward fulfilling his boyhood dream of owning a farm, outbidding the Vanderbilt farm of Biltmore, North Carolina, the Crocker farm of California, and others to purchase Flying Fox, "the greatest bull of modern times," at the annual Cooper sale of imported Jersey cattle at Coopersburg, Pennsylvania. Lawson made the winning bid in front of "5000 people, comprising most of the noted breeders of America and many from Europe, including John A. Perrce, secretary of

Left: Figgis, shown here, represented just a small portion of one of the world's most impressive herds of Jersey cattle. (Photo by T. E. Marr) Below: Miles of Kentucky fence ringed the estate, running past the Dutch-style windmill and dove cote. (Photo by T. E. Marr)

At any time, dozens of horses could be seen moving about the estate, at work, or at play. (Photo by T. E. Marr)

the Jersey Island Jersey Association." His longest-lasting opponent, Mrs. Patterson of Pennsylvania, bowed out as Lawson raised the price to $7,500. Making twenty-three other purchases that day, Lawson stole the show. According to the *Scituate Light*, "It is the consensus of opinion that Mr. Lawson's new Dreamwold farm, by his purchases at this sale and the importations he has just made from the islands, starts equal, if not superior in quality to any Jersey herd in the world." By mid-June, the cows, led by Flying Fox, started to arrive at their new home. By August, his prize racehorse, Boralma, had reached Dreamwold.

Left: With an estate as large as a small village, Lawson felt the necessity of including a set of fire trucks as part of the Dreamwold layout. (Photo by T. E. Marr)
Below: Dreamwold manager George Pollard lived in his own house on what is now Curtis Street. (Photo by T. E. Marr)

Writers from around the country descended on the estate, each scouring his thesaurus for new descriptors apropos of what they had seen. "Aladdin's lamp would be a poor substitute for Mr. Thomas W. Lawson's check-book in this practical age," wrote Maurice Baldwin for *The House Beautiful* in April 1903, "when illusions must be produced with stone and wood and beautiful metals, and no dreams seem worth the having that cannot be expressed in paint or marble, or by the subjugated graces of exquisite but illiterate nature.

"Rather is this an age, indeed, of illusions made permanent, when a Midas-fingered business man can, with a stub-pen, invoke the genii of art and labor to the realization of dreams strong enough to have lived

Below: Cottage No. 7 still stands today at the corner of Curtis and Branch Streets and Country Way. (Photo by T. E. Marr) Right: The main gate to Dreamwold, at Egypt, offered a hint to the traveler that something unexpectedly wonderful was about to be experienced. (Photo by T. E. Marr)

through the din of foundries and the sardonic chuckle of a stock-exchange ticker."

E. C. Lincoln, in *The National Sportsman,* wrote, "Today the United States abounds in magnificent estates and the beautiful homes of our wealthy families grace the hillsides and the vales of thousands of our towns and hamlets. It is not of the city houses that this article is to speak, but of the country residences, the gems of beauty tucked away in rural places far from noise and bustle, and the battle and strife of the busy world. Superior far to any city block, magnificent though it may be, these are the places which permit of a free scope for the artistic temperament, an unlimited chance for exercise of the love of the grand and the beautiful.

"Our eastern states abound in these magnificent tributes to the taste, genius and refinement of America's men of wealth.

"Massachusetts has its full share, and among them, preeminent in its perfection of loveliness, one shines forth supreme.

"It is of the latest conspicuous creation of this class that this article is to speak in particular. It is of Dreamwold . . . an enchanted fairyland, the creation of a man's genius, pluck, and indomitable persistence. He took a piece of bleakest New England, a barren and sterile territory, covered with stones and rocks. This he transformed into a paradise."

Remarking on Lawson's early order that every facet of the estate should "be heavy, strong, simple and quiet," *The Architectural Review* commented, "The farm has been laid out on this basis and everywhere you will find the Dreamwold badge; stamped on the leather of the books, burned into the furniture, worked in silk on the blankets and linen, formed in brass on the horse equipments, stenciled on the farm wagons, painted on the palace stable cars and on the office sign; engraved on the farm stationery; everywhere the Dreamwold badge, a winged horse held by the strong hand of a man, and symbolizing, 'Beauty, Strength and Speed.'"

Lawson soon recognized the grandeur of his own creation. In December of 1903, after a dispute over taxes in Cohasset, he abandoned that town forever, making Dreamwold and Scituate his permanent summer home.

Left: Another set of gates, on Branch Street, framing Lawson Tower in the distance, allowed workmen another means of access to the estate. (Photo by T. E. Marr) Below: Lawson would not have built his farm without an opulent farmhouse. (Photo by T. E. Marr)

Chapter Three
A Comfortable Country Home: The Dreamwold Farmhouse

When Tom Lawson first conceived of Dreamwold, he had no intention of inhabiting it for half of the year. According to his original thoughts, Dreamwold would be an escape for his family, a place to entertain in the summer. He spared no expense in building it, though, even with sporadic use in mind. He made sure that he and Jeannie and their children would have a comfortable, homey house, filled with beautiful things. As with everything else on his estate, all the way down to his horses, the main farmhouse held the qualifying name Dreamwold, derived from the rolling countryside, a "wold" or undulating plain in Anglo-Saxon, and, of course, their "dream."

The curving drive to Dreamwold Hall showed a sprawling, low-slung Dutch Colonial building, with a central section that had a chimney at either end. "Not a castle, stern and forbidding, not a great stone pile, standing sentinel challenging your approach, but a house, and such a house, pleasant, inviting and homelike, speaking comfort and happiness in its every aspect." (Lincoln, p. 511). Two smaller wings flanked the main hall, attached by windowed passageways. The central section was reserved for the family, with one wing off a conservatory passage for guests (to the left), and the opposite wing for the kitchen and servants' quarters. In all, Dreamwold Hall contained twenty-two rooms. Four large hot air furnaces burned 175 tons of coal in the winter to heat the entirety of the livable space.

This house was to be a farmhouse, both lavish and simple. All the many details reflected that theme. Lawson's vision, insight, and love of beauty drove the implementation of all these details. He said to his architect, "I want everything to be beautiful but it must be as unostentatious as it is possible to make a comfortable country home." In later years he added a portico to the main facade, with a double chimney also added to the house directly above it. A large carved rooster near the top separated the stacks, placed as though holding them together. The rooster merely reinforced the farm theme.

Upon entering the front door of the main hall, visitors immediately felt welcomed, surrounded by serenity and peacefulness. The great entrance hall ran from the front to the back of the house in one unbroken span, affording a view of the terrace, from which could be seen a panorama of the Atlantic Ocean with Minot's Light to the north, Duxbury to the south, and the beautiful layout of the farm in the immediate foreground. Inside, the dining room stood to the far right and on the left, the living room. All of these rooms could be thrown open to make one large space for entertaining large groups of guests.

Off the living room, the connecting conservatory led to the guest wing with its billiard room and library. Above it were the guestrooms (also known as the "Bachelors Quarters"). The other wing, off the dining room, had a large butler's pantry connecting to the kitchen, equipped with an

The simple Dutch-Colonial style of the Dreamwold farmhouse belied the fantastic visions that would be gathered by visitors within its walls. (Photo by T. E. Marr)

A Comfortable Country Home: The Dreamwold Farmhouse

Below: The main entrance hall, shown here, opened to the dining room to the right, at the back of this image. (Photo by T. E. Marr) Right: Looking across the entry hall, the stairs to the second floor can be spied. (Photo by T. E. Marr)

old-fashioned Dutch oven, built specifically to satisfy Lawson's lifelong penchant for Boston baked beans, baked the old-fashioned way, and all up-to-date appliances. Servants' rooms and storage areas comprised the rooms above the kitchen.

In the hall, high backed cane chairs with leather cushions arranged against the walls of green maple panels added to the feeling of comfort. Brightly colored oriental carpets, paintings, sculptures, and other artwork enhanced the welcoming atmosphere of the room. Above, between the beams, the ceiling was painted a celestial blue. Appropriate carvings and friezes carried out the farmhouse theme, with fruits, vegetables, and specific Dreamwold animals all exuberantly displayed.

This sense of subdued splendor spilled into the other rooms. Light from the large windows gave an airy aspect. Each room offered a different color to the wood paneling, each defining a slightly different theme. The hall woodwork displayed a green black, the living room a green gray. The dining room held a sandalwood color, due to a special acid bath given to the wood. Over the dining room table dangled a magnificent chandelier crafted by Tiffany and Company in

in the shape of a large pumpkin, with its attendant blossoms and vine. A smaller pumpkin blossom light over the breakfast table lit the adjoining alcove, as pumpkin blossom wall sconces lined the room. Pumpkin carvings on the wood around the fireplace, and corn carved above the wall panels helped complete the picture. All around, a series of fruit and flower designs, all hand colored and executed by the best artists, delighted the eyes. Crescents about the room were painted in oils, each showing some farm scene, while a frieze around the room showed the Dreamwold farm in an uninterrupted sequence. Large cinnamon bear and tiger skin rugs complemented Oriental carpets on the floor. Above the bar, a majestic carved and painted peacock reposed in all its splendor.

Here, too, could be found a mantle clock designed by Lawson himself, made entirely of teak with carvings surrounding the face. On one side stood Lawson Tower; on the other,

The dining room boasted a Tiffany pumpkin globe lamp, a Grueby vase above the fireplace, and andirons personally designed by Tom Lawson. (Photo by T. E. Marr) Below: The pumpkin globe lamp came complete with its own vines and blossoms. (Photo by T. E. Marr)

Below: The modern kitchen of the main farmhouse had to have a Dutch oven in which could be prepared Tom Lawson's beloved baked beans. (Photo by T. E. Marr) Right: Holes in the floor around the water-driven pipe organ acted as a speaker system, to transport the sound from the pipes held below. (Photo by T. E. Marr)

his Dutch windmill. A carving of the Lawson Pegasus emblem crowned the work. Lawson paid more than $3,000 to have it built. Years later, prominent Scituate businessman Allan Wheeler rescued the clock from Clarence D. Collin's Clock Museum in Georges Mills, New Hampshire. Wheeler, who had an abiding love of all things Scituate, displayed the clock at Scituate Federal Savings Bank in Scituate Harbor, where it can still be seen today. In the fireplace silently rested a pair of bronze andirons, also designed by Lawson and forged by Russell Crook, standing bronze bears, one enjoying his honey, the other beset by stinging bees. They were, of course, an allegorical reference to Wall Street.

A comfortable living room with a music area at one end housed not only a grand piano, but also a full-pedal water-driven pipe organ, the pipes for which were located below the organ in the basement. Carved representations of Bacchus, of Greek mythology, and bunches of grapes formed part of a frieze around the room, interspersed with portrayals of many of Lawson's favorite animals. The whole was

held together by garlands of foliage and flowers delicately colored. Murals painted by Vesper George, known for his Boston art school, adorned the walls.

Here, the wedding ceremonies for his daughter Gladys' Autumn Wedding (October) and daughter Dorothy's Snow Wedding (December) took place. Lavish decorations of flowers, fruits, and greens appropriate to the seasons, all obtained from the farm and lovingly designed by the farm staff, made these occasions memorable.

Some of Lawson's vast collection of elephants were displayed here as well. When speaking with a writer for *Pacific Monthly Magazine* in 1911, Lawson said of collecting miniature pachyderms, "Yes, it is one of my fads. I have over three thousands elephants. They are of jade, ivory, bronze, teakwood, and almost every other kind of material. One of them is over 2800 years old and came from the 'Forbidden City.' It was part of the loot taken during the Boxer Rebellion." Full appreciation of the value of this collection can be realized when it is revealed that Lawson hired a man especially to count the elephants on a regular basis, to make sure that none were missing. One time, in the middle

More Grueby vases adorned the fireplace mantle in the living room, shared with some of the Copper King's favorite elephants, an ocelot rug, and a mural of some of his prized farm animals. (Photo by T. E. Marr) Below: The conservatory passage connected the main house with one of its wings. (Photo by T. E. Marr)

of the night, this gentleman was awakened to do his job because Lawson thought he heard a prowler, thankfully a false alarm.

The conservatory, located between the main building and the guest wing, had a domed ceiling of hand painted tiles. Potted palms alternating with figures and animals of bronze lined the walls. Flowers bloomed everywhere. Jeannie loved flowers, and at Dreamwold she could enjoy her passion for them everywhere in the house.

Next came the billiard room with its polished beams and theme of green, green corduroy cushions, carpeting with green figures, and green flowered wallpaper. A "combination" billiard table and all the comforts for which a person could wish made this a lavish retreat. The fireplace fascia depicted the legend of Captain Kidd, who was said to have buried some of his treasure under a huge linden tree on the Dreamwold property. The tree stood beside the paint shop on the grounds, still there sometime after the estate was sold, when entrepreneur William Chase had his animal farm near that location.

The library was a handsome room lined with bookcases. Beautiful carvings in the woodwork reflected a literary theme, with busts of famed writers peering out from wall sconces. The ceiling featured an astronomical chart, also painted by Vesper George, with a border of the signs of the zodiac and the four seasons in the corners. Carved gnomes representing history, leg-

In the billiard room, elephants on the mantle shared the space with a Remington statue (on the bookcase), and paintings by the great masters of art. (Photo by T. E. Marr)

end, printing, and other like subjects danced on a frieze around the room. No one gnome looked like another. Gnomes also looked down from the square lanterns that lit the room.

Upstairs, the bedrooms were almost as opulent. A vast amount of white brought out the hand painted tiles from the Grueby Pottery Works, depictions of rabbits and "benighted" children surrounding the rooms. Mrs. Lawson's bedroom shone in silver and gold. The Gorham Manufacturing Company of Providence, Rhode Island, made her sterling silver dressing table and bench for the Paris Exposition of 1900, constructed from 1,080 troy ounces of silver. The bench used an additional 173 ounces. It took over a year to

Far left: On the walls of the stairway to the bachelors' quarters, Teddy Roosevelt and George Washington share equal space. (Photo by T. E. Marr)

Photographer Thomas E. Marr caught the library before it had been completely stocked. (Photo by T. E. Marr)

A Comfortable Country Home: The Dreamwold Farmhouse

Below: The wall sconces in the library displayed the faces of some of the world's great writers. On the right is William Shakespeare. (Photo by T. E. Marr) Right: Such a farm as Dreamwold offered endless decoration possibilities at harvest time, the dining room here dressed for the autumn wedding of Tom and Jeannie's daughter Gladys. (Photo by T. E. Marr)

build, the company awarded the Grand Prix for design and execution at the Exposition. Lawson bought the set for Jeannie at the retail price of $8,800 for the table, and another $960 for the matching stool. Nothing was too good for her.

Yet even with the stately magnificence of Dreamwold Hall, Lawson and his wife required an even safer sanctuary. "He saved the most important thing until a year after Dreamwold Hall was thrown open. On the exact spot where his wife used to sit in her carriage and admire the view, he had built a cozy cottage-like house that he named The Nest. A gate through the fence at one end of the farmhouse gave access to it, and it was solely a place where he and Mrs. Lawson could find relief from the excitement attendant of large parties in Dreamwold Hall."

When Jeannie died in 1906, Lawson was inconsolably devastated. Thinking she was improving in health, he had let his daughters sail for Europe. Telegrams bearing the grim news of her death recalled them and their honeymooning brother Arnold. He could not bear to have her body buried, and kept it in The Nest in a hermetically sealed coffin for several days, while he had a stone tomb built nearby. Built on the grounds of The Nest, Lawson called it The Rest. He spent long hours by himself at The Nest, mourning her loss,

many weeks passing before he felt himself able to return to "business."

The roof of the tomb was a single slab of granite weighing sixteen tons brought from the famous Quincy, Massachusetts, quarries. Lawson felt the mausoleum must be a fitting tribute to Jeannie, so beautiful granite benches were placed around it with newly planted mulberry trees for shade. Later, the mausoleum was relocated to nearby Fairview Cemetery, behind the First Trinitarian Congregational Church, when the Dreamwold estate was sold.

Stepping back from these buildings, the visitor plainly saw how the farmhouse and The Nest formed part of a larger whole, how their design and construction complemented the stables and work buildings, coming together to make Dreamwold Farm one of the most spectacular country estates in the United States. "The general impression after a tour of 'Dreamwold'—the house and the grounds—is of a virile joy in nature and simple living, richly but restfully expressed." (Baldwin, p. 312)

With his farm now completely laid out, Lawson could concentrate on ancillary projects, and the details that would take Dreamwold from one man's estate to a showplace for the world.

In the dining room's breakfast nook, one Remington statue stands in the window, while another settles for the floor. The wall sconces, designed to complement the pumpkin globe, shed light on the special silver punch bowl and table designed for the Hull Yacht Club. (Photo by T. E. Marr)

Chapter Four
For the Benefit of Half the County: Lawson Tower

Just when Tom Lawson learned of the Scituate Water Company's plans to build a 276,000-gallon, seventy-five-foot-high steel water tank across from his Dreamwold property is unclear. The proposed water tank would be directly in view of his new home, and would dominate the landscape at Scituate Center. As early as 1899, though, he sent an architect to Europe to study design ideas to beautify the metal standpipe, and, in effect, the local area. What stands today is the result. Known as the most beautiful, most photographed, and the most expensive water tower in the United States, Lawson Tower was designated an American Water Landmark by the American Waterworks Association in 1974 and listed on the National Register of Historic Places in 1976.

The Portland Company of Portland, Maine, completed the tank in 1901 for the Scituate Water Company. Lawson, disliking the looks of the tank, gained permission to have it enclosed by a wooden structure which would be distinctive and give pleasure to the eye. He would pay for these "improvements," including a ten-bell chime system and clock, a bill which ultimately totaled over $60,000.

Coolidge and Carlson, an architectural firm of Boston, designed the Romanesque structure, which included a bell room, a clock room with dormers, an outside spiral stairway in its own enclosure, a console room, and a carved masthead at the top. The structure was made entirely of wood, surrounding the metal tank but not touching it, a specification the Scituate Water Company insisted upon. The distance between the tank and the wooden trusswork at the base measured just eight to ten inches. Landings at each fifteen feet of elevation facilitated cleaning and painting of the tank.

Constructed by the Charles Logue Co., the tower was completed in 1902. When finished, it stood 153 feet tall from the base to the top of the masthead. Copper finial balls placed atop each dormer, the masthead, and the chime console room gave testament to Lawson's demand for detail. The structure also reflected Lawson's superstitious belief that the number three brought good luck, as several dimensions of the building are divisible by that number.

Built to resemble a medieval watch tower, the design of the tower might have drawn inspiration from Stahleck Castle on the Rhine River, Bacharach, Germany. A belfry above the water tank housed a ten-bell chime. Open to the weather, the bell room was surrounded by large window openings (now screened), the floor sheathed in copper to protect the water tank below, which was open at the top.

As with any construction site, danger was ever-present during the tower's construction. During the final weeks of the project, as the staging surrounding the tower was being removed, a young workman sadly fell to his death, toppling from approximately one hundred feet and fracturing his skull on the ground below, on June 24, 1902. (*Annual Report of the Officers of the Town of Scituate*, 1902, p. 64) Despite this unfortunate event, work continued as planned.

The Meneely Company of Troy, New York, manufactured the bell set, weighing 11,100

Lawson's neighbors at the First Parish Church at Scituate Center looked on in awe as his "Observatory Tower" was being constructed in 1902. (Photo by T. E. Marr) Below: Shortly before completion, the sun shines down through the open-roof framing of Lawson Tower. (Photo by T. E. Marr)

For the Benefit of Half the County: Lawson Tower

pounds. The chime of ten bells ranged from 25.25 to 52 inches across. The bells themselves were stationary, clappers struck against them to make their sounds. At first, the largest bell, weighing 3,000 pounds, did move, fixed on its own wheel mount. This system did not prove practical, so it, too, was made stationary. Long chains connected to each bell could be manipulated by levers in the console room to play musical selections. Concurrently with the installation of the bells, E. Howard & Company put in a clock with a timing mechanism on the next level above the bell deck, enabling the bells to strike the hour and to ring the Westminster Chimes each morning and evening. A speaking tube located in the console room enabled the player to hear the bells directly and also to converse with anyone above.

The bells were ready for use just before July 4, 1902. The August 22, 1902 *Scituate Light* reported that "Arthur Pepper has secured the position of Chime-ringer. The chimes are to be rung every evening from 8 o'clock until 9 and three times on Sunday." South Shore residents as far away as Cohasset enjoyed the bells for their beautiful sound, and on a summer evening could sit on the porch or in the yard and hear those soothing sounds of the Westminster Chimes or an occasional concert.

Most people enjoyed the bells. However, there was at least one complaint of record, noted in the *Scituate Light*, December 11, 1903. "The chimes of Dreamwold are not for ragtime tunes, and Arthur Pepper, 'chimist,' must confine his evening concerts to music of a more dignified character. Mr. Pepper, who discourses music an hour each evening for the benefit of half the county, has fairly well covered several books of gospel hymns, exhausted a large part of the familiar ballads and made familiar many others. Recently he essayed some innovations, but 'Under the Bamboo Tree' was evidently considered too frivolous to

Opposite: Lawson's inspiration for his magnificent tower probably came from an architect's drawing of Stahleck Castle on Germany's Rhine River. (Photo by Betty Miessner) Below: When Lawson Tower was completed, the eyesore of the Scituate Water Company's steel standpipe had been hidden forever. (Photo by T. E. Marr)

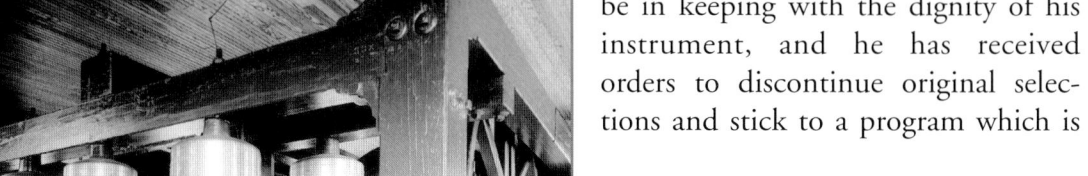

The newly installed ten-bell chime could be played from a console room approximately eight stories below. (Photo by T. E. Marr) Far right: Three wrought iron hinges supported the extreme weight of the heavy door to the tower's spiral staircase. (Photo by T. E. Marr)

be in keeping with the dignity of his instrument, and he has received orders to discontinue original selections and stick to a program which is daily submitted." The complaint may have come directly from Lawson himself, as no other person would have power to issue "orders" to Pepper.

Two years later, as reported in an undated article saved in a scrapbook now in the possession of the Scituate Historical Society, Pepper struck again. "Mr. Pepper, chime ringer of the Dreamwold bells, has once more gone in for frivilous [sic] stunts, and the chimes are flooding the night air with music of a distinctly secular character. For about two years the hour from 8 until 9 in the evening has been devoted to a concert by the bells of Dreamwold, and this nightly concert has become through habit almost a necessity to the people within five miles of the chimes . . . Mr. Pepper usually plays a programme which is daily submitted from headquarters, but it appears that certain evenings are left open to his option, and recently he has improved these evenings by displaying the scope of his repertoire.

"'Sweet Marie' has been flung wide on the breeze, to the delight of the frivilous [sic]. Similar tunes have been played until it would seem that the

Far left: Lawson's attention to detail could be seen in the ball finials atop the turrets, the mast carved to look as if it were shingled, the diamond shingle details, and the added return detail of corbels. (Photo by Charlotte Parsons) Left: Even after Lawson had passed on, tunes rang out from the tower's chimes. Here, circa 1930, Fred Bailey plays a selection from the console. (Photo by Josephine Schuman)

term *chestnut bells* might fairly describe his instrument. Last night, however, a comparatively new and unseasonable number was rendered, and, in defiance of the weather the chimes rent the air with 'In the Good Old Summer Time.'"

The tower's observation area presented wonderful views of the surrounding countryside. Climbing 123 steps—a number divisible by three—from ground level to the bell deck, Scituate Selectmen John J. Ford, Thomas F. Bailey, and W. H. Varnell enjoyed the view the week of August 25, 1902, at Lawson's invitation. Were it a clear day, Massachusetts' North Shore would have come into view; to the east they might have seen Provincetown on Cape Cod, before the construction of the Pilgrim Monument. From the sea, mariners relied on Lawson Tower as a landmark, making it a valuable navigation aid.

As early as 1908, the town showed its appreciation to Lawson for his positive impact on the community. On March 2 they voted to "abate the tax of Thomas W. Lawson on

Below: A 1930s lightning strike caused a fire to break out on the roof of the tower, calling for subsequent repairs. (Photo courtesy of George Bearce)
Right: Over the years, the bell chains on the open-weather observation deck corroded, prohibiting the use of the console. Here, Richard Burt, who liked to play barefoot, manipulates the chime chains from above. (Photo by Charlotte Parsons)

Beauty, Strength, Speed: Celebrating 100 Years of Thomas W. Lawson's Dreamwold

the Water Tower and Egypt Post Office." (*Annual Report of the Officers of the Town of Scituate*, 1908).

The process that brought Lawson Tower under the ownership of the Town of Scituate began at the March 5, 1923 Town Meeting, when a bill of sale was presented and $3,500 voted to buy the clock and the chimes from the now near destitute Lawson. The Town then purchased Lawson Tower from the Scituate Water Company in 1931 after having signed a 99-year lease at the 1929 Town Meeting. The Town used water from the tank until 1988, when leaks developed. The tank was then drained, and its use discontinued. Strong interest in keeping the tower as a landmark and tourist attraction resulted in having the Scituate Historical Society administer the structure for the Town, showing it at open houses, for school groups, and scheduling chime concerts. On hundreds of occasions during her three-decade tenure as president of the Scituate Historical Society, Kathleen Laidlaw trudged up the stairs with schoolchildren, cautioning the children to hold their flashlights and to "walk carefully and stay in line."

Far left: Longtime Scituate Historical Society President Kathleen Laidlaw led countless schoolchildren up the 123 steps of the tower, herself known to ring the chimes quite frequently. (Scituate Historical Society collection) Below: The weathering of the chains led to a concurrent deterioration of the console, shown here prior to restoration. (Scituate Historical Society collection)

In probably the largest, most expensive bicentennial project of the local area, the Town of Scituate paid for the reshingling of Lawson Tower in 1975. (Photo by Charlotte Parsons)

Selectman Jackson E. Bailey remembered the dedication needed to keep the clock and timing mechanism in working order, telling the story of one of the men employed by the Town to take care of the weekly chore in his book *Tell Us a Story, Jack!* "When I became selectman, we hired Benny Turner to wind the clock. After he had climbed the 121 [sic] steps each week for two years, he came to the selectmen's meeting one night. He wanted more money, not because he was tired of the job, but, he said, 'Because I'm getting a lot of kidding around town. All the boys say I have the best legs in the country, including the Rocketts, from running up and down those stairs!' We gave him a raise, mostly because we couldn't find anyone else to do the job."

Over the years, the chains stretching between the bell deck and the console room deteriorated, and the bells could no longer be controlled by the levers below.

For many years, Scituate resident Richard Burt rang the bells on special occasions by pulling on the bells chains on the bell deck, most notably doing so on Christmas Day with appropriate selections such as "I Heard the Bells on Christmas Day," "Joy to the World," and others. In the summer of 1979, volunteer Don Hodgkins played the chimes on Monday evenings from 7:30 to 8:15, and most recently, Lennea Badger worked as chime ringer. Laidlaw always tried to have the bells rung for any special occasion, including ringing in the New Year herself. In 1992, Eagle Scout Joe Jaymes III com-

Left: The reshingling of the tower included double courses and hand cutting of flared shingles at the base. (Photo by Charlotte Parsons) Center: No detail was left out, as even the carved mast and finial were refurbished by workmen secured by safety lines. (Photo by Charlotte Parsons) Below: Considering their exposure to nearly a century's worth of seaside weather, the bells have held up well. (Photo by Rudolph Mitchell)

*Below: A structural assessment in 2000 found major deterioration in the bell support structure. (Photo by Paul Miles)
Right: For safety purposes as the tank removal process began, the bells were removed and relocated to a storage facility in Cincinnati, Ohio. (Photo by Paul Miles)*

pletely refurbished the chime control room to its original beauty.

Because of natural weathering, the Tower has been reshingled at least twice in the last one hundred years, in the late 1930s and in 1975. The water tank was still in use at that latter date, so the work had to be done very carefully. The distinctive flair of shingles at the bottom of the tank was retained, with double courses extending half the height of the tower, the job including the roof as well. Cutting these shingles proved to be labor intensive, as each one had to accommodate both flair and curve.

Remarkably, through the years the tower has not sustained significant damage from storms and lightning. On Sunday, May 30, 1939, however, lightning struck the tower during a thunderstorm, resulting in a shingle fire on the conical roof at about the one hundred-foot level. The Scituate Fire Department, using their new pumper and a hose carried up inside, soon had the blaze extinguished. Firemen lugged the heavy hose and nozzle up all 123 steps of the spiral stairwell, laden with all the necessary equipment in what must have been an exhaustive, atypical emergency response. Today, a lightning arrester averts such an occurrence from happening again.

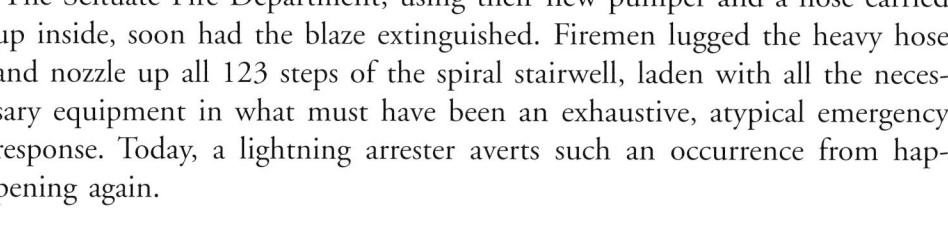

Beauty, Strength, Speed: Celebrating 100 Years of Thomas W. Lawson's Dreamwold

Currently the tower cannot welcome guests to the bell deck, as the bells have been removed for safety and restoration. The wooden supports and the metal bolts holding them together had deteriorated to the point where the bells, if rung, could have fallen, causing much damage both to themselves and to the tower. One very cold day in December 2000, the Verdin Company of Cincinnati, Ohio, removed the bells, which are now safely in their care, to be restored, and installed ready to ring when the bell frame is made structurally sound once again.

Following a detailed architectural and structural survey in mid-2000, the Scituate Historical Society presented the Town a four-year plan for restoration and repair of the tower, expected to be approved pending availability of funds and grants. The rusting water tank will be removed, pending a vote of the Town, and may already be gone by the time this book comes to publication. For safety reasons, to both workers and the tower, this work must be completed before the bells can be returned to their rightful place. Once they are returned, Scituate will once again hear the sounds that Tom Lawson brought to the South Shore, echoes from the past that will forever be synonymous with the legacy of the Copper King.

Left: The weight of the bells and the narrowness of the stairway necessitated the use of a crane to remove the bells. (Photo by Paul Miles) Below: In any season, the beauty of Lawson Tower shines through. (Photo by Charlotte Parsons)

Chapter Five
A More Simple and Lovable Crudity: Tom Lawson Speaks His Mind

By March of 1903, Thomas W. Lawson's Dreamwold had become Scituate's greatest single topic of conversation, pushing aside most of the memories of the tragic winter storm of November 1898. That storm, the Portland Gale, which had thrown the Boston pilot boat *Columbia* ashore at Sand Hills, destroyed a thousand barrels of Irish moss, and changed the course of the North River, taking the lives of three young local men in the process, stood for nature at its worst. Lawson's estate represented rebirth, life, and growth, its overflowing gardens, deer park, and unrivaled coterie of the world's finest farm animals promoting nature's glorious side.

The people of Scituate came to be proud of the fact that within the borders of their town rested one of the country's best-known and best-stocked farms, and many, though not all, looked up to Lawson as a great benefactor. They marveled at the estate from outside its many miles of fence, and lined up to tour the grounds for Wednesday open houses. Lawson extended personal invitations to many groups, including all of the local chapters of the Daughters of the American Revolution.

Controversy arose, though, in that month of March 1903. Shortly after a Scituate Town Meeting an anonymous "Visitor" penned a letter to Floretta Vining, editor of the *Scituate Light*, one of Vining's nine South Shore of Boston newspapers, complaining about the behavior of the manager of Dreamwold. Vining published the letter, "He Should Be Banished" in the Arena column of the March 20 edition.

"Editor of Scituate Light:

"Could any one who worked for another have more enemies than the man who is superintendent for Mr. Lawson at Egypt?

"Perfectly devoid of tact he walked up the aisle at the recent town meeting and handed out a letter. Mr. Lawson will never have his noble motives appreciated as long as he has a common laboring man, devoid of education and manners at the head of his business. The place is entirely beyond him; he belongs in a cow stable. There are men on that estate that are a king to him, in the most menial positions.

"Mr. Lawson everyone admires, and especially his thoughts and ideas for the grand old town of Scituate, and when he has any more business with the town and its people let him do it himself. To a man they will take off their hats and do his bidding.

"Can there not be a man secured for the position as head of Mr. Lawson's farm who can at least speak the English language and who has some knowledge of the faintest rules of etiquette? All last summer visitors would go to see Dreamwold and as this bear was the person they came in contact with, it was a great ordeal to go through with, to have to encounter him.

"Dreamwold is a show place and a constant comfort to all visitors to the South Shore, but it will never be the success it should be as long as such a common person has anything to do with it.

"Mr. Lawson deserves something better than the opinions formed by strangers after visiting the farm.

"He should be banished to where he came from, for prosperity does not agree with him, his rise and progress have been more than he could stand.

"A VISITOR."

With land set aside for even wild animals, Dreamwold truly defined nature at its most beautiful. (Photo by Lester Hobson)

A More Simple and Lovable Crudity: Tom Lawson Speaks His Mind

Endless paths meandering under rose arbors and over rustic bridges made Dreamwold a wonderland of natural beauty. (Photo by T. E. Marr)

Lawson wasted no time in responding to the letter. The following week Vining's nine newspapers ran a two-column "Open Letter From Thomas W. Lawson" that spoke not only to the question of his manager's abilities and manners, but to several other topics Lawson wished to share with the people of the region. The letter is a classic example of Lawson's fantastic command of the English language, penchant for run-on sentences, and ability to convey his thoughts and emotions in dramatic fashion with paper and pen.

"One of your correspondents last week sent you a communication which I feel calls for a word from me," he begins, "a word for the good of Dreamwold, the enlightenment of all good citizens of Scituate and the peace of mind of any of those citizens who from any cause are looking for trouble with Dreamwold, its people or its owner, and before saying my word I would most respectfully and emphatically try to impress upon every one, whether a citizen of Scituate or not, who may have ought to do with Dreamwold, that while I am anxious to avoid trouble and discord, I am equally anxious when it comes along with a chip on its shoulder, to give it the most active kind of wrestle imaginable."

Immediately, Lawson lets the "Visitor" know his thoughts. "I once wrote, and have liked it ever since, 'Fools wrangle; wise people pick daisies and make snow men,' meaning any one who does not like what the other fellow is doing can always find great big fields far removed from the other fellow's bailiwick where he can pick daisies in summer or build snow men in winter and cause no one, himself included, unhappiness." If the "Visitor" was discontented with anything he saw at Dreamwold, he could simply stay away from the grounds and traverse the earth until he found a place that did make him happy.

Lawson then opens his comments to address the entire interested population of the area, stating emphatically his intentions behind the construction of his enormous farm. "I did not build Dreamwold for a public place or a show place in any sense of the word," he writes, responding directly to the "Visitor's" comments, "but, on the contrary, as a home for myself and family and our pets, and for our pleasure and happiness only; in fact, as the most private place possible, to which I could go to get away—absolutely and completely get away—from the many people who for reasons of their own chase me 'from pillar to post' with this project and that scheme until I almost pray for that delightful state of freedom which was once mine, but alas! is forever gone; that state which goes only with obscurity and lack of riches."

Once planted, Lawson allowed his plants to freely grow. (Photo by T. E. Marr)

He realized, too, though, that his comments might seem harsh and even selfish, but felt that he was completely within his rights to speak them. "I know it is too bad to say it, and in saying it I may break the charm and lay myself open to criticism, but in honesty, I must say it! If the public will only leave me to myself I won't object to anything they think of me or my affairs. When I planted the pretty things at Dreamwold I did it not to meet the approval of visitors, but because I and mine liked them. When I put my beautiful chimes in Dreamwold tower I put them there that my people could listen to their sweet music. To be sure, I hoped hundreds, or thousands, who were less fortunate in worldly goods than myself could enjoy them, too, but I deserve no credit for that, as the governing desire was a selfish one—purely and simply a selfish one."

Through the construction of his estate, the Copper King, perhaps unconsciously, was acting out his assigned role in Victorian society. Whether he felt his farm should be a public spectacle or not, he knew it would be. Moreover, he made it so by inviting guests from as near as the Chief Justice Cushing Chapter of the Daughters of the American Revolution to as far away as

The once stark-looking utility poles had blended with the landscape by 1903. (Photo by T. E. Marr)

Tom Lawson valued his employees, or his "people," as he called them, even more than his prize animals. (Photo by T. E. Marr)

the German Agricultural Society to tour the grounds, even establishing a pass system at the guard house for bug-eyed day-trippers interested in taking in the grandeur of his creation. As neatly stated by gardening historian Michael Weishan in *The New Traditional Garden* (p. 60), "Victorians loved to see and be seen." A man of his wealth and flamboyance could be "seen" through his buildings and gardens without personally being physically in view. Lawson, who sought to have both a new breed of carnation and the world's largest sailing vessel carry his name, obviously had a strong desire to be recognized.

Nevertheless, Lawson continues his correspondence with the people of Scituate and the surrounding towns with rather direct and surprising honesty. "First and last my thought was, Dreamwold is and always will be a place where I . . . can wander about without being compelled to listen to the stories of its beauties or my 'cuteness' in creating them, which are really as 'headachy' to me as the things others are compelled to listen to when they have done things all wrong."

Lawson authorized an annual manor party for his employees to show his appreciation for their work. (Photo by T. E. Marr)

Eventually, he comes to the defense of his hired hand, the manager whose actions aggravated the "Visitor" to the point of writing a letter of complaint to the local press. But his response to the accusations is not one that could have been predicted. "Your correspondent is right—my manager, Mr. Pollard, has no tact, is not polite. Your correspondent is right, he did walk up the aisle at town meeting without a 'By your leave,' for he knew that if he attempted to present my letter in any other way there would be a new manager for Dreamwold. I do not require of Mr. Pollard or any of Dreamwold's people tact or smoothness; I only insist upon honesty, loyalty and fair treatment of all with the fairness tempered to the poor or unfortunate. No, Mr. Pollard was not responsible; I, and I alone am responsible for everything connected with Dreamwold."

Lawson's unwavering public support of his manager through the 1903 letter marked the beginning of two decades of open and unbreakable loyalty to those of his "people" who believed in and followed his creed of "honesty, loyalty and fair treatment of all." Later that year he introduced another tradition that endeared him to his staff, as described in the December 4, 1903 edition of the *Scituate Light*. "Mr. T.W. Lawson, whose large estate at Egypt, give him almost baronial possessions, is fittingly the first citizen of Massachusetts to introduce a time-honored English custom of giving his dependents a grand ball. The English gentry throw open their country houses for the entertainment of the tenantry, usually during the Christmas holidays, and owners of large industries often engage some country place or inn, where they give a banquet attended by their employees in their company. Mr. Lawson employs a force of 150 people at Dreamwold, and was anxious to inaugurate this pleasing custom there and choose Thanksgiving for the occasion as this is the most cherished holiday of New England." He gave instructions to just let the staff have some

Even a fast-moving Lawson employee had trouble getting his name on a dance card. (Scituate Historical Society collection)

fun, no matter what the cost. "The orders received by Mr. Pollard, manager at Dreamwold, were: 'Let the boys run the dance and musical entertainment to suit themselves, and let each man invite a friend and have as good a Thanksgiving time as the place will stand, and the estate pays the bills."

Years later that support of his workers manifested itself in the flying of a special flag above Dreamwold Hall showing one star for each member of the estate's work force that had left to fight for the country in World War I. So his spirited defense of Pollard comes as no surprise. "The best answer I can give to the accusations your correspondent made against Dreamwold's manager is to say: After the exercise of my best judgment, for I recognized from the start the heavy responsibilities of the position, I selected from among scores of capable men Dreamwold's present manager, and there has never been a day since that I did not congratulate myself on my selection."

Figuring that he had the ear, or eye, as the case may be, of the people of Scituate, Lawson next warns them of the consequences of major complaints and objections about his doings, and intrusions on his family's privacy. "I would impress upon the citizens of

Scituate that Dreamwold asks no favors of any one. It did not come into their midst to be a burden to them, but rather to be something they would welcome and be proud of. What belongs to Dreamwold the citizens of Scituate can be assured Dreamwold will get, unless I choose to forego in the interest of Scituate and her citizens the getting of it; and if at any time I come to the conclusion the getting of it is too disagreeable, too fraught with uncomfortableness or unhappiness for myself and people, Dreamwold will quietly and sedately fold itself up and go back to the farming region it was before Dreamwold was created. This may not seem to many feasible or even possible, but I can assure them it would not cause me one millionth part the thought or labor to bring about this condition of affairs that was necessary in creating Dreamwold."

Lawson's cold, stormy temper when faced with such unpleasantness had shown itself during his attempt to send his yacht *Independence* off to defend the America's Cup in 1901. When his efforts proved unsuccessful, ultimately being excluded from the race by the New York Yacht Club, he defiantly ordered that the beautiful vessel be stripped plank by plank. Its mast ended up as a flagpole on Planter's Hill in Hingham, part of the Trustees of Reservations World's End Reservation. There could be no doubt that if crossed, Lawson would take Dreamwold away. "One thing the citizens of Scituate can rest assured of: Whenever—and the Lord forbid that time will ever be—an insurmountable difference arises between them and Dreamwold, there will be no wrangling or feeling shown in its settlement, for I have too high respect and admiration, for the town and its stalwart citizens to ever let my affairs be the cause of discord."

Lawson saw the entire event caused by the correspondence as a challenge, one that he could easily take on without fear of loss of any kind. In fact, he saw it also as an oppor-

Visitors to Dreamwold first checked in at the office building at the main gate. (Photo by T. E. Marr)

tunity to share some of his personal beliefs, and in so doing, gives readers even today another example of why even though disliked by many people for his straightforward manner, his work force always remained by his side. "It happens to be my good fortune to be able to talk honestly to the citizens of Scituate, or anywhere else for that matter, for in starting to 'kick' through this vale of trouble and crisscrossness I adopted for my motto, 'I'll give favors, not take them.' And I have been able in all kinds of weather to adhere to that motto, and I teach it to my people. I try to impress upon them that the jewel of jewels is independence. To be sure, you cannot get far in what is called society, or politics, or many other walks of life where truckling and crawling upon all fours is the requisite, but you can get in all those places where the air is pure and the ozone plenty, and you can always be sure when you go to bed you will get the sleep that comes only to the free; to those possessing the knowledge that if they should awake in the Great Unknown they can face their Maker and answer, 'You made me in your image, and I come to you in that image, erect and not bowed from constant creeping on all fours.'"

As a grand finale to his open letter, Lawson reveals why Dreamwold ended up in Scituate and not elsewhere, in almost poetic fashion. "In having this frank discussion with the people of Scituate, I trust that they will bear in mind what I say should be taken in a different spirit from those things which they have been in the habit of listening to from politicians or those who have some ulterior end in view; that they will remember I did not locate Dreamwold in Scituate for their votes, for freedom from taxes, or for any such possible advantages; I did not build Dreamwold in Scituate because of anything Scituate's people had which I wanted, but simply that I might share with them those things which are so plentiful in their town, so plentiful that all may have their fill without depriving any one of their share, the good things of nature which belong to all alike, to the rich and the poor, the driver and the driven, in equal proportions if they but care to take them; because I knew the cosey beauties which nestle in Scituate's hollows and rest upon Scituate's hills; because I knew its tangled briars and wild roses were a bit more tangled and lots wilder than in other nearby nooks of nature; that the green of the ocean was a shade greener and its white caps a mite whiter off Scituate's coast than elsewhere available, and that her fishermen and her mossers were in a more simple, mossy and lovable crudity than in any other place that had these other beautiful things of nature in combination. These were the things that brought Dreamwold to Scituate."

    Controversy came to town with Tom Lawson and rode with him as a traveling companion for the rest of his life. No less should have been expected for a man with as much determination to reach his goals as Lawson held. His passion for his family, his "people," his pets, and the beauty of nature drove him to want the best in life for them all, and as he had the financial wherewithal to attain what he desired, nothing could stand in his way. Despite his claim that he would take Dreamwold from Scituate if pushed, Lawson would stand toe-to-toe with the locals on future issues, but none ever came to be so serious as to make him disappear.

Beauty, Strength, Speed: Celebrating 100 Years of Thomas W. Lawson's Dreamwold

As early as June of 1901, Lawson felt it necessary to establish a pass system to the Dreamwold grounds. In later years, only one man, preacher Billy Sunday, dared hop the fence to get to the Copper King. (Scituate Historical Society collection)

Chapter Six

An Emblem of Victory Birthed From Suffering: The Story of Lawson Common

Tom Lawson could be a harsh enemy to face. Poised like one of his English bulls whenever unpleasantness reared its ugly head, he stood firmly ready for any challenge. Conversely, if he considered someone to be one of his "people," or embraced them for any other reason, he spared no energy to see that they received all that they deserved in life. Both of these sides of his personality showed themselves during the two-decade battle to bring about the construction of a Civil War monument in Scituate, a project which struck deep chords within his heart.

Lawson's father Thomas, then a forty-year-old Cambridge carpenter, enlisted with Company "F" of the Third Regiment Massachusetts Volunteer Cavalry on August 27, 1862, heeding President Abraham Lincoln's and Governor John Andrew's call for additional troops to fight the Confederacy after the bloody battles of the early summer had proven to the Union government that the war would not indeed end in ninety days, as originally believed by most residents of the Northern states. Mustered in two months later, on October 27, the senior Lawson rode with the Third for four years, being wounded at the losing battle at Sabine Cross Roads outside Natchitoches, Louisiana on April 8, 1864, one of eighty-two Union casualties that day. As one of the original draftees of the unit (which began as the Forty-first Regiment Massachusetts Volunteer Infantry), he was mustered out in Washington, D. C., on May 20, 1865. He died soon thereafter. At war's end, young Tom Lawson was just eight years old.

"My father was a soldier," he revealed to the people of Scituate at the dedication of the town's Civil War Monument on June 17, 1918. "The four years in which he fought and bled and at the end of which he died so seared my childish heart with war's terrors, so etched my boy's soul with the thrills and inspirations of war's romance, that every time I hear the fife and drum and see a Grand Army uniform I vision times and deeds beyond the ken of the peace-born-and-reared."

Lawson was still working on purchasing land for his estate when he began to put his plan in motion to memorialize Scituate's soldiers and sailors with a monument of their own. At a special Town Meeting held on April 5, 1902, the townsfolk "Voted that the Treasurer be authorized to convey to Thomas W. Lawson for the consideration of $1.00 a quit claim deed of land known in the town as the Common, between Branch, Willow [now Beaver Dam Road] and Central Streets [now First Parish Road], reserving therefrom enough land for a Soldiers' Monument." (Scituate Town Archives: C-1 p. 534) The previous year the town had given Lawson permission to make improvements to the same lot of land, then still under the ownership of the town.

In 1737, the gore of land described as the Common in the 1902 Town Report became home to the First Parish Church. Two previous incarnations of the church had been built at Scituate Harbor in 1634 and 1682, on Meeting House Lane. This church, the third, had been built there as well in 1708, but moved, as public demand called for it to be at the center of town. The move made the name Scituate Center not only geographically-significant for that particular village, but, as the uncontested home of government, education, and religion for the town, it became the community's nerve center as well. The third structure remained until 1774, when the church acquired new land and built the "Old Sloop" a few hundred yards to the west on what is now First Parish Road. Townsfolk used the "Old Sloop," a building so grand that mariners used its steeple as a navigational aid at sea, for town meetings during the American Revolution, as soldiers drilled on the now empty common land across the way. Even without a church standing on it, the people of Scituate still

The Old Sloop, long a landmark at Scituate Center, burned in 1879. (Lester Hobson photo of an unattributed painting)

referred to the triangle of land where the First Parish Church once stood as the "Old Meeting House Lot" or the "Church Common." (The Old Sloop burned in 1879, replaced the following year by the fifth and current First Parish Church that stands in the shadow of Lawson Tower.)

The deed did not pass into Lawson's possession until February 27, 1907. By that time, his life had dramatically changed. His wife Jeannie, the only love of his life, had passed away on August 5, 1906. The shock brought on by her death left him unable to continue with his business interests. Instead, he had moved into The Nest to mourn in private, leaving his subordinates to carry on his work. The Common land remained unimproved, and somewhat forgotten, for the next eight years.

Finally, at Town Meeting on March 1, 1915, the Scituate selectmen instructed moderator Henry Turner Bailey to appoint a "Committee to consider the erection of a Soldiers' and Sailors' Monument in Scituate," eventually comprised of Grand Army veterans Thomas F. Bailey, James L. Prouty, and John H. Towne and artists James Hall and William H. North, with the moderator serving as a non-voting consultant. Also a member of the Park Commission with North and Walter S. Harrub, who had made headlines thirteen years previously for his renegade alcohol prohibition enforcement methods on behalf of the town, Henry Bailey had coauthored that year's report of the Park Commission. "An article will appear in the warrant for the next Town Meeting relative to a certain parcel of land at Scituate Center, formerly a part of the Town Common, which, in the judgment of the Commission, should

Once one of the tallest structures around, the First Parish Unitarian Church stood in the shadow of Lawson Tower. (Scituate Historical Society collection)

The remaining members of George W. Perry Post No. 31, Grand Army of the Republic, long desired a monument to their fallen brethren. (Photo by George E. Lawrence Company)

The son of a Civil War veteran, Lawson, here shown with G.A.R. member Francis B. Lee, stood by their side in their fight for a monument. (Scituate Historical Society collection) Right: After the town settled its arguments pursuant to the monument's design, Lawson made sure that everyone, including his own grandchildren, had a grand time at the dedication. (Scituate Historical Society collection)

be held by the Town as a public park, and as a site for a memorial to the soldiers and sailors of Scituate."

According to Scituate historian Barbara Murphy, the decision process for the design of the monument did not go smoothly. "The dwindling numbers of the Civil War veterans had long desired such a monument so commonly erected in other communities, and finally a committee of three Grand Army of the Republic veterans and two artists were to plan a monument. But agreement among the committee members was impossible—the veterans and artists engaged in heated controversy about what would be appropriate. The emotions of the town's people were wrenched as they empathized with the aged veterans and the cultivated tastes of the artistically trained."

The following spring, with Bailey again serving as moderator, the town voted on March 6, 1916, "That the Committee on Soldiers' Monument be continued; that it be requested to solicit subscriptions for its erection; that when such subscriptions reach $3,500 the Town now agrees the sum of $6,500 will be added thereto for that purpose, and that the Park Commissioners be instructed to take under the provisions of Chapter 28 of the Revised Law and Acts, in amendment thereof and added thereto, the same land conveyed to Thomas W. Lawson by the Town of Scituate, by deed dated February 27, 1907, and recorded in Plymouth County Registry of Deeds, Book 965, page 518, called 'Old Meeting House Lot,' or 'Church Common.'"

The vote to take Lawson's land back from him

awoke a sleeping giant. The Copper King unleashed a verbal tongue-lashing on the local politicians the likes of which has never again been seen, and kick-started the process that culminated with the dedication of the Civil War monument.

"Gentlemen - Now that the Scituate hot-air artists, who annually in Town Hall paint atmospheric pictures of how tax-payers should be stomach-pumped for the benefit of themselves, have had their 1916 lung-fest and have hung their word-balloons across their ribends, I would have a word with you, papas of this town.

"Fifteen years ago, I expended some $2,000,000 turning tin-canned, ash-enameled rock piles into rare shrubbed and rosed Dreamwold.

"Since then I have distributed between $100,000 and $200,000 each year in seeing that it did not slip back into its former state.

"In that time I have paid our town each year some $7,000 in taxes.

"In that time I have never registered kick, robust or feeble, at the fact that the town treated my estate as woodchucks do the harvest of the unfortunate who plant in their midst.

The day's program featured several stirring and patriotic speeches. (Scituate Historical Society collection) Below: As the Civil War veterans dedicated their monument, another global conflict was raging across the Atlantic. (Scituate Historical Society collection)

An Emblem of Victory Birthed From Suffering: The Story of Lawson Common

Although it had its detractors in town, the new monument on the old church common certainly made an improvement on the landscape. (Scituate Historical Society collection) Right: Once the home of the First Parish church, then a drill field, and later a buffer zone for the Lawson estate, the common ended up as a gathering place for the people of Scituate. (Scituate Historical Society collection)

"I furnish my own fire protection, street watering and cleaning, sewerage, lighting and insect destroying.

"I do not use town schools, and whenever the town's roads around my estate become dangerous or impassable, I pay the town for repairing them or build new ones.

"In the beginning I was held up by the town's thrifties to the score of thousands. To protect my entrances I foolishly paid silly prices for land; still I refrained from leg exercise, but when I found myself about to spend rising $100,000 upon that part of the estate adjoining Beaver Dam gate, where the town's plot might be turned into a public pig emporium after my expensive beautifications were complete, I refused to go ahead with purchases and improvements until the plot was deeded to me.

"I consider the plot worth $30,000 and the town may have it at that price and good ridance [sic], but at any less—not until the last court in the land has passed upon the affair.

"As to the eminent dough-maining of it—my lips are cracked and it is not nice of those warm-air artists to make me laugh. I do not mind saying to you, Town Papas, that hell will be encrusted with a thick coating of congealed atmosphere before that plot is thoroughly 'eminently dough-mained.'"

Keeping his quill well-inked, Lawson next wrote to the remaining members of the Grand Army that if the town should buy the land from him, he would turn over all $30,000 for the veterans' monument fund; if not, he would give the G.A.R. the land with $500 for the monument, with one stipulation. He wanted a promise that the G.A.R. would never sell the land back to the town for less than his valuation of $30,000. In May, the town acted on its eminent domain threat. Lawson deeded the land to the veterans, accompanied by $500 in gold coins, tucked inside a small casket built for the purpose. That same month Henry Bailey attempted to have the monument committee expanded by two seats. After a spirited and vehement protest by Thomas Bailey, the selectmen voted against the idea.

In late October 1916, Scituate's internal battle made Boston newspaper headlines. Due to Henry Bailey's national ties to the world of art, a wide selection of proposal drawings and models had been received for discussion by the monument committee, including submissions from such well-known sculptors as Anna Ladd, Hugh Carns, Herman Matzen, and even Augustus Lukeman, who would later complete the work on the Confederate memorial at Stone Mountain, Georgia, when the project's originator, Gutzon Borglum, left to begin Mt. Rushmore in South Dakota. The five-man committee studied the designs, with the three Grand Army veterans souring on all the entries but one, which they felt fully represented what their monument should be. The artists violently disagreed. So

An honor roll of World War II veterans later joined other monuments on the common. (Scituate Historical Society collection) Below: The elephant fountain on the common has undergone several changes over the years. (Scituate Historical Society collection)

Below: An enormous boulder moved from a local farm became the basis of a First World War memorial. (Scituate Historical Society collection) Right: Mortars stand guard at the western end of Lawson Common. (Photo by John J. Galluzzo)

heated was the discussion and so set were the veterans on the choice of Quincy's James Craig's design, that James Hall and Henry Bailey resigned from the committee in disgust.

"We felt that the thing should be judged by merit, and certainly it was not," Hall told the *Boston Traveler* on October 24. "The design which has been selected is commonplace and is lacking in distinction. In my opinion it does not accord with the specifications. On top there is an eagle which is so large that it is out of proportion." The design he and the other artists had voted for "was a remarkably beautiful shaft 80 feet in height, quite original and altogether a striking thing. It would have been one of the most striking monuments in the state. It contained a dignified figure of a cavalryman at the foot as required in the specifications, and which harmonized well with the shaft." One sculptor, unnamed by the *Traveler*, stated that the eagle on the Craig design looked like "a vulture with the pleurisy."

Sculptor Craig, though aware of the comments of the artists, nevertheless reacted to the news that his design had been chosen "like a wild man," in his own words. "Those artists shouldn't have quit the committee. That is a schoolboy way to act. They should stick. The world loves a game loser." Coincidentally, Craig had previously been awarded the contract to design the Thomas W. Lawson Mausoleum. Although there is no recorded proof of any previous discussions to the effect, the rapid choice of the Craig model by the men of the Grand Army and Lawson's recent history with the sculptor may have decried a predetermined selection made by Lawson and the veterans.

Henry Bailey vowed that day to call a special town meeting to stop the project cold. By October 26, ten Scituate petitioners had taken the matter to Plymouth County Superior Court, where an injunction was granted restraining the committee from awarding the contract to James Craig to build the monument. A hearing was scheduled for November 6. Scituate Deputy Sheriff John Turner delivered the news to the veterans that they would be required to appear in court by surprising them at their monthly dinner meeting, in what Lawson described as "the most rottenest way you could ever guess!"

Always ready for a fight, Lawson put pen to paper once again, on October 30, in what has become known to Scituate historians as the "Town Papas Letter." The ensuing scrum essentially pitted nouveau-riche Lawson against a strong force of Scituate "townies" (residents who had been born and raised within the borders of the town), although Lawson also took up issues with summer visitors to North Scituate. Siding with the veterans, he remarked that the "shoresurfites," as he called them, "don't know any-

Playful elephants delight children of all ages as the common's centerpiece. (Photo by Sally Maish) Below: The eagle atop the monument, described by one sculptor as looking like "a vulture with the pleurisy," has nonetheless stood the test of time. (Photo by John J. Galluzzo)

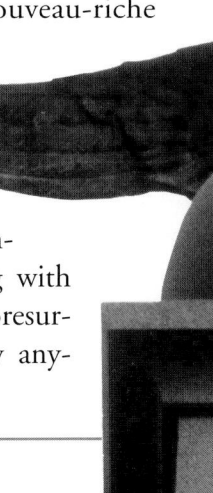

thing about how a Vet feels about a memorial that is going for all time to mark how he and his dead comrades fought for Old Glory and dear old Yankeeland. (No, they didn't know any more about how the old Vets felt than the old Vets know about stay-at-home-and-peddle-liquor-at-war-prices patriotism.)

"So they had a statue made out of clay," he continued, "with a North Scituate girl in shoresurf tights and said she was the Goddess of Liberty, and another of a First Cliff dude and a Sand Hills masher, both in the skinniest bathing togs ever, and they said one was to represent the Navy and 'tother the Army, and all three were to be holding a giant cigarette-shaped flagstaff with a sign on the flag, 'When you smoke, get the Dizzy Lizzy Cig. It's artistic and there are no others.'"

In a few uncertain and heretofore uninvented terms, Lawson let the target of his venomous wrath know what they could do with their selected design. "And now, Dear Town Papas, if you don't mind taking it hot from the grid, it would please me to hand you this both-sides-buttered bit of wisdom: Send for the shoresurfites and sweetly, but firmly convey to them the information that they may take their artistic statue and set it up, say, on the sands at Marshfield, just one town to the south

Scituate Civil War veterans demanded that a sailor be represented with equal billing alongside a foot soldier on the monument. (Photo by John J. Galluzzo)

of Scituate; or they may take it and set it up on the ledge of Cohasset, one town to the north of Scituate; or they may set it up on a stout raft-floater and anchor it to Bizzenbuck Rock, three miles oceanward to the east of Scituate; or they may set it up on Toppintit Hill, in the town of Norwell, four miles to the west of Scituate; or they can set it up in Hell, way, way to the leeward of Scituate; but under no circumstances can they set up their artistic boomer in Scituate, under the pretense that it's a soldiers' monument."

At a special town meeting held on December 13, Moderator Henry Webb appointed William W. Wade to replace James Hall on the committee, a move that made no impact on the final outcome of the fight. County commissioner Frederick Bailey, Henry's brother, suggested that the town could not even discuss the construction of a monument on land not municipally owned, and proposed building it on the town land recently made vacant by the moving of the 1893 high school. With that necessary bit of procedure out of the way, John Turner submitted a written motion suggesting that the committee "SHALL

Neither a "First Cliff dude" nor a "Sand Hills masher," the soldier on the monument instead represented the ideal chosen by the Grand Army men. (Photo by John J. Galluzzo)

submit designs to a jury of sculptors. When the meeting drew the 'shall' teeth and inserted 'may,' which means nothing at all, Mr. Turner withdrew his motion." Another citizen resubmitted the motion with the altered language, and the motion passed by a vote of 134 to three. The veterans would have their monument.

Tempers cooled during the winter, as the 1917 Town Report recorded that not only did the town vote $10,000 for the erection of a Soldiers and Sailors Monument on March 12, but at a special town meeting on June 22, 1917, the town voted to accept a portion of land at the Common deeded by Lawson to the town for the construction of the monument. When asked if the town should authorize the Monument Committee to locate and erect the monument on that land, the townsfolk voted unanimously to do so. The famous Olmsted Brothers of Brookline, Massachusetts, designed and planned the landscaping of the park at a cost of $154.34. Lawson took control of the project, and within a year's time, the monument was dedicated.

On June 17, 1918, the town paid solemn tribute to the "memory of those who fought from '61 to '65." Prayers preceded selections by the Marine Band from Bumpkin Island Naval Training Station in

There could be no denying the love expressed by the people of Scituate for their veterans of the War of the Rebellion. (Photo by John J. Galluzzo)

Quincy Bay, the unveiling of the statue by Miss Jean Lawson, and speeches by the many invited dignitaries, including Scituate Selectmen Charles W. Peare and Ansel F. Servan; State Representative Walter Haynes; Thomas F. Bailey, Chairman of the Monument Committee; George W. Wilder, Senior Vice Commander, Dept. Massachusetts, G.A.R.; Sergeant Parker H. Litchfield, 151st Depot Brigade Detachment, Medical Department; Congressman Joseph Walsh; and Massachusetts Governor Samuel Walker McCall.

As could be expected, Lawson's words again stole the show. Any animosity he had held for the town had disappeared, and he turned his full attention to the last few members of the Grand Army, and the irony of dedicating a Civil War monument as American soldiers fought in the Great War across the Atlantic. "Think what the unveiling of this emblem of victory birthed from suffering, from misery, from war's horrors, will mean to the legion of youth now on the way 'over there' where Democracy is locked in mortal struggle, where its deadliest foe, Autocracy, is in its death throes! Think

The park has expanded to include tributes to veterans from all of America's major wars, including World War II. (Photo by John J. Galluzzo)

how it will bring home to our soldiers and sailors of today the truth, 'God battles with the right!'

"This whole damnable cataclysm . . . is not war. It is a masquerade in the name of war . . . it is the duty of all of us to do all we can and in every way we can to aid in killing this hideous thing; to aid in killing it so dead that it can never come to life again."

When the "war to end all wars" came to an end, the town granted permission for a Welcome Home Committee, chaired by Lawson, to "erect a suitable tablet and to beautify the Church Common in honor of the Participants of World War I." No fight arose in connection with this proposed memorial. On July 4, 1919, when peace was once more upon the land, Lawson again led a great celebration, a grand affair with the presentation of medals, speeches, bands, and the opening of Dreamwold Park for further entertainment.

"At your Committee's first meeting it developed that nothing would satisfy our grateful townspeople but a celebration which would surpass that

The town's Vietnam War vets have this stone to look to when remembering lost comrades. (Photo by John J. Galluzzo)

of all other communities in the country of equal size of Scituate; we should have a large memorial tablet with fitting mounting in a park where nature's beauty would splendidly set it off, we should have on Independence Day a grand unveiling with music and oratory and from the unveiling the assembled masses should march to an all-day festivity and then from a great building holding 5,000 people there should be presented to all our returned sons and daughters by orators of national repute the most beautiful bronze medal possible and to the parents and dear ones of those who went but did not return, an equally beautiful gold medal."

The Committee moved an eighty-nine-ton boulder two miles from the Mitchell Brothers' Farm on Hollett Street, placing it on the site and fastening a memorial tablet to it at a cost of $935. Lawson commented "At the start-off its moving was considered impossible, but owing to the fact that the Town has an Archie Mitchell, who by the way gave the boulder, nothing of a like nature is impossible."

In 1919 the park was just about complete with a round pool in place, walks installed, and plowing and grading accomplished. The pool sported at its center a wonderful and distinctive fountain of three little elephants, part of Lawson's personal contribution to the project. He also donated from Dreamwold, "fifteen of my prettiest approximately thirty-year-old elms . . . planted in the best possible positions," with forty-two more to be shipped from a Framingham nursery.

And so on June 13, 1919, the town voted unanimously "to accept that portion of the Church common at Scituate as a gift from Mr. Thomas Lawson to be used for Park and Memorial purposes." They then voted that "the thanks of the

Scituate's Korean War veterans are remembered by this stone marker. (Photo by John J. Galluzzo)

An Emblem of Victory Birthed From Suffering: The Story of Lawson Common

meeting be extended to Mr. Lawson for his generous gift to the Town." Thus, the two parcels of land that made up the park were united once again, under the name "Memorial Park."

By 1920 the landscaping firm of Morrison and Gillis, under the guidance of Mr. Lawson, completed the Park with the $8,000 the Town had voted (plus what Mr. Lawson provided) for that purpose. Soon after, the Board of Selectmen and the Grand Army secured two large trench mortars from the United States Government and placed them at the point of land where First Parish and Beaver Dam Roads meet. Assistant Veterans' Agent Lawrence Langley refurbished those same mortars in 1989.

On March 7, 1921, as a gesture meant to erase all ill feelings between the copper magnate and the people of Scituate, the townsfolk "Voted that the town of Scituate name the park bounded by Central, Branch and Willow Streets, Lawson Park," (Scituate Town Archives C-12 p. 570) giving a standing ovation to Lawson as a sign of respect and appreciation.

Other improvements such as curbing (1924), memorial boulders to those who served in World War II, Korea, Vietnam, and on

Now more than a decade old, the Desert Shield/Desert Storm marker commemorates Scituate's veterans who fought in the Persian Gulf in the early 1990s. (Photo by John J. Galluzzo)

Operations Desert Shield and Desert Storm, and a boulder placed in memory of Scituate's police and firemen have been added to this beautiful piece of land. The elephant fountain plantings have been redesigned and refurbished, the entire layout beautifully maintained by the town.

Most importantly, the townspeople use the park, appreciate its beauty, and care deeply about the monuments there. Pranksters have toyed with the elephants, painting them pink, and then again in polka-dots, and even stealing one, which was quickly found. But even today, three quarters of a century away from the death of its benefactor, the elephant fountain sprays water in the summer, Memorial Day speeches waft through the air, and the children of Scituate run and play with youthful abandon in Lawson Park, unencumbered with the weight of the emotion, sweat, and tears that defined the initial design of the park that today bears the name of Scituate's most famous resident.

Lawson Common also has room for the town's public service officials. (Photo by John J. Galluzzo)

The enormity of Dreamwold farm can truly be understood through this contemporary bird's-eye-view architectural drawing.

Chapter Seven
Larger Than Life

The days have long passed since an interested listener could ask someone who knew Tom Lawson whether or not a story told about him on the street were true. Lawson dominated his time and place, an unique individual whose personality inspired stories by the hundreds. The following collection of anecdotes and tales represent just a small portion of what has been said and heard about the Copper King in Scituate over the last hundred or so years.

One day, soon after Tom and his family had settled at Egypt, an acquaintance came up to him and greeted him effusively, saying, "Tom, I'm so sorry that I have not been to visit you at Dreamwold." Tom replied at his most genial, "Think nothing of it, if we'd wanted society, we'd have gone to the North Shore [of Massachusetts]!"

Tom Lawson was a very superstitious man. He believed that the number three brought good luck. His office on State Street was number 333, his office phone numbers were 333 and 339, and any construction of buildings frequently had measurements that could be divided by three or multiples thereof.

One notice in the June 13, 1902 *Scituate Light* reported, "The Marie Theresa had a very successful fishing party on Monday last, catching about 200 pounds of cod and haddock. As they were ready to come in, Captain M. E. Labrador sighted the Dreamer [Lawson's expensive motor yacht] in the distant east sailing up to the boat. One of the boys waved a rock cod to Mr. Lawson. He immediately called for the engineer to stop the boat, which he did, and Mr. Lawson took the cod."

Lawson once paid a Boston florist $30,000 for the privilege of naming a newly developed hybrid carnation "The Lawson Pink." Ever after, he always had a "Lawson Pink" in his buttonhole.

It took famous Swiss watchmaker Edward Koehn a full year to build Lawson's famous pocket watch, at a reputed cost of $10,000. An inch in thickness and nearly four inches from stem to base, it was a work of art. A portrait of Lawson and three of his children adorned one side, while on the other was a depiction of Mrs. Lawson and the other three children. The crown of the watch was set with a semi-precious stone that was green by daylight and red under artificial light. A special feature rang a chime automatically fifteen minutes before the stock market opened and fifteen minutes before it closed. Precisely at 7:45 p.m. it chimed to remind Tom to walk the dogs. He believed this watch to be his good luck charm and always tried to have it with him on special occasions. The only time his charity horse, Boralma, lost a race—the Kentucky Derby, no less—Lawson blamed himself. He had forgotten to bring his watch. On only one other occasion did he not have it with him. Testifying before a Congressional hearing about charges he had made concerning insider trading, he was unable to construct a convincing argument. After that episode, Wall Street ceased to fear him or be guided by his advice. This event may possibly have been the beginning of his financial decline.

Tom never did anything by halves. He designed and had made by Tiffany and Company a massive sterling silver punch set which he presented to the Hull Yacht Club. It was called the "Lawson Cup" and consisted of the punch bowl, ladle, tray, and eleven cups, all resting on a specially made table carved in the like design of the trophy. There was an elaborate ornamentation of a schooner under full sail in the rough seas, the handles half figures of Neptune and Venus, eleven dolphins decorating the base. The name *Lawson Cup* was in relief. Each of the cups had mermaid handles and were ornamented with high relief reproductions of various winning America's Cup yachts with their winning dates. The

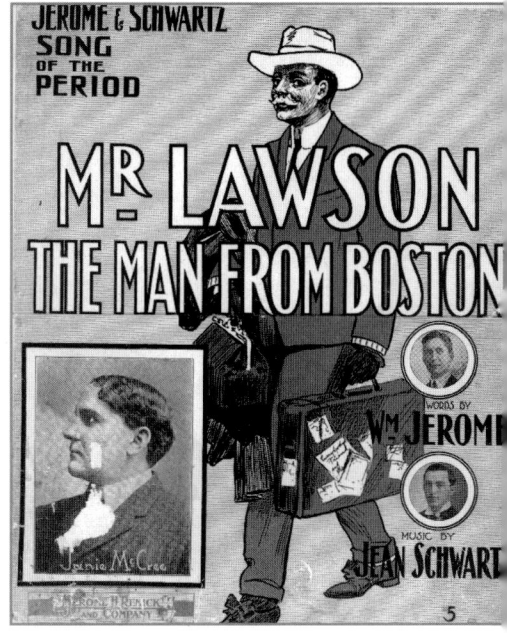

If he had any doubts beforehand, Lawson had to know he had reached the top when people began to write songs about him. (Scituate Historical Society collection)

Although the master has gone, the Dream lives on. (Photo by Elise Walters)

And though the original judges' stand has disappeared, this near exact replica stands at the entrance to the Dreamwold condominiums in 2002. (Photo by Elise Walters)

tray, with like designs, had engraved on it, "This cup was presented by Thomas W. Lawson to the Hull Massachusetts Yacht Club to be raced for by ninety-foot sloops in the year 1901."

A year or so after Mrs. Lawson had died, Tom took his family and a group of friends to Europe. They arrived in Monte Carlo and, of course, had to play at the Casino. Tom, in an unheard of streak of luck, broke the bank. The Casino had to close for the rest of the evening, as there was no money left in their coffers. The next day Tom doled out his winnings equally to each of his friends and family members and told them to spend it—all of it—in Monte Carlo. He wanted the money to stay in the country.

Writer Willard de Lue of the *Boston Globe* always had some stories about Lawson to tell:

"At the height of Lawson's fame, when his story of 'Frenzied Finance,' an attack upon the stock-manipulations by financiers whom he called 'the system' was

When he found out that Egypt needed a new post office, Lawson simply built one. (Photo by T. E. Marr) Right: One of the first controversies to strike the Lawson estate concerned the firing of the local postmistress. (Photo by T. E. Marr)

Beauty, Strength, Speed: Celebrating 100 Years of Thomas W. Lawson's Dreamwold

still a sensation, he accepted an invitation to be the principal speaker at an annual civic banquet of the Peoria, Ill. Creve Coeur Club, Feb. 22, 1906.

"As the day approached he set out from Boston in a private car, accompanied by a battery of reporters who wired stories of his progress. At Albany the regular connection was missed. A special train was made up, and a wild pursuit undertaken. Failing to catch up with the train ahead, the Lawson Special ran through to Chicago, where a delegation from Peoria was on hand to accompany their guest to his destination.

"Next day Peoria lionized Lawson. Crowds acclaimed him. And at 6 o'clock, when the banquet began, 800 men were at tables in the big Coliseum (which was decorated with thousands of Lawson

With time as his most valuable asset, Lawson arranged for a New York, New Haven, and Hartford Railroad train to take him directly to Boston every morning. (Scituate Historical Society collection) Bottom left: A mile race track added to the awe-striking experience of Dreamwold. (Photo by Lester Hobson) Below: Short-tailed horses had their own stables at Dreamwold. (Photo by Lester Hobson)

Once the retreat of Tom and Jeannie Lawson, The Nest is today a private home. (Photo by Elise Walters)

Beauty, Strength, Speed: Celebrating 100 Years of Thomas W. Lawson's Dreamwold

Left: In June of 2002, Lawson Tower turned a century old. (Photo by Paul Miles) Corrosion affecting the standpipe inside the tower has caused concerns for the Town of Scituate for the safety of the structure. (Photo by Paul Miles)

Pinks), and the galleries were crowded with spectators, largely women.

"At 7 o'clock the speaking began, and with speech and song the hours dragged on in what soon became a smoke-filled hall. A railroad president spoke. Adm. Schley spoke. Two congressmen added their voices. One of them, down for a 20-minute talk, told funny stories for well over an hour. On and on it went.

"Not until 11:55 was Thomas W. Lawson introduced to a weary, yet wildly cheering audience.

"He stood until the clamor subsided—though down at the back of the hall some of the bibulous boys were a bit noisy.

"'I'm going to tell you a funny story,' Lawson began in his high-pitched voice. He was not an orator, but unlike

Scituate had never known such opulence before the arrival of the Copper King. (Photo by T. E. Marr) Below: No dog show was complete in the first decade of the twentieth century without entries from the Lawson kennels. (Photo by T. E. Marr)

some orators, he always said something.

"'I'm going to tell you a funny story about a man who came 1000 miles to make a speech . . . and didn't.'

"He was sorry, he said, but he didn't feel that he could go on. And it wouldn't be fair to his audience. 'What I have to say you can read in the morning paper.'

"Then he sat down."

Tom had the world's largest flagpole erected on his estate, 166 feet in height, carved from the tallest tree to ever leave the state of Oregon. The weight of the wood broke a plank on the Fore River Bridge in Weymouth on its way down the coast from Boston.

In 1908 he raised a pennant that read, "Roosevelt and Taft," flown on the day the Republican candidate was to be nominated at Chicago. Lawson believed the convention would stampede to Teddy Roosevelt, but if it didn't, his flag would represent that Taft stood for the president, and Lawson would

When the New York Yacht Club blocked his opportunity to race his yacht Independence for the America's Cup, Lawson had the vessel stripped plank by plank. (Scituate Historical Society collection) Below: Following and enjoying his many passions, Lawson dressed appropriately for every situation, even yachting. (Scituate Historical Society collection)

Below: For safety purposes, the Town of Scituate called upon the Verdin Company to remove the bells. (Photo by Paul Miles) Right: Once removed, the bells were taken to Cincinnati, Ohio, to be restored and stored until work on the tower's bell frame had been completed. (Photo by Paul Miles)

Beauty, Strength, Speed: Celebrating 100 Years of Thomas W. Lawson's Dreamwold

Left: Once the bells are restored, they will be played from the beautifully-restored console room. (Scituate Historical Society collection) Below: Many of the Lawson buildings still stand, including this cottage at the corner of Country Way, Branch Street, and Curtis Street. (Photo by Elise Walters)

support him just as strongly.

The world's largest sailing ship, the *Thomas W. Lawson*, carried his name up and down the East Coast. Lawson wrestled with the number of masts it should have, finally consulting his lucky pocket watch for advice. Although his watch rang out six chimes in the darkness of a restless night, he decided on seven masts, the only time he went against the advice of his watch.

Mariners warned Lawson that with thirteen letters in its name the ship would be cursed, but he paid them no mind. In 1906, he tempted fate again, publishing *Friday the Thirteenth*, a novel about the stock market. Then, on Friday the thirteenth of December

An estate the size of Dreamwold deserved the world's tallest flagpole. (Scituate Historical Society collection) Right: Shown from the rear of the farmhouse, the star-spangled banner flies at Dreamwold. (Photo by T. E. Marr)

1907, on her first transatlantic voyage, the *Thomas W. Lawson* wrecked in the Isles of Scilly, killing all but two men in her crew.

In the last days of his life, when Tom was confined to bed at The Nest with diabetes and Dreamwold was being sold, one of his good friends (who was also a Trustee of the Estate) came to him with some money that had been found in a cash box that no one had known was there. Even Tom was mystified how it got there. The amount was $550 in bills. The Trustee said to him, "This sum will hardly do your creditors any good. Why don't you take it and buy yourself some comforts while you are ill."

Tom immediately had a direct telephone line to Wall Street installed by his bed. He enjoyed himself playing the Market. Six weeks later he had parlayed that money into $40,000 which he promptly gave to his children. He died within days.

To the very end, he kept his Midas touch.

A man with an active mind, Lawson, shown here in his Boston office, reveled in the thrill of the pursuit of his goals. (Photo by T. E. Marr)

Larger Than Life

Lawson's lucky elephants delight children all summer long. (Photo by Sally Maish)

Postscript

One hundred years after the construction of the Dreamwold estate, and seventy-seven years after his death, Thomas W. Lawson's voice resonates through the air at Egypt and Scituate Center. His powerful persona has left a legacy for the town, one that will not easily disappear.

After the big estate auction in October 1922, the property and buildings of Dreamwold were put up for sale by Trustees Horace T. Fogg and William A. Burton. According to the Scituate Assessors Records, in 1927 Frank and Elfreida Dailey bought the hall, laundry, paint shop, and judges stand along with the racetrack, deer park, dove cote, another house, and garage, all coming with acreage. Dailey, a successful Boston lawyer, may have been the one who added the beautiful ballroom at the back of the house. The Dailey's owned the hall until 1934.

Entrepreneur Bernard Killian bought it and turned it into a restaurant in 1952. He and his family ran it until George Viola and George DeMarco bought it in 1956. They kept it for only a few months with Lewis Ward as manager. Then, in 1957, Ward, along with partners William Degan and John O'Connor, bought the house and business. They owned and operated Dreamwold for the next twenty-six years. In time, the restaurant became less profitable, so they turned successfully to catering weddings and other functions. Many current Scituate residents remember having a grand time at high school dances, musicals, and one-act plays at the Hall.

Rising from the depths of poverty, Tom Lawson chased his dreams to the top of the world. (Photo by T. E. Marr)

Other portions of the vast property were sold and single family houses built. However, the well-built roads were retained and used by developers, including George E. Kimball & Son Co., of Hingham and R. M. Bongarzone of Scituate. In 1926, the Children's Sunlight Hospital bought the farmhouse by the Branch Street Gate, creating Sunlight House, a summer retreat for the blind, welcoming clients from the city for many years. After passing hands several times, it too was converted to condominiums in the 1980s.

In the back of the farmhouse, near the duck pond, William Chase had his wild animal farm, quite an attraction in the 1930s. After Chase sold his business, it became Benson's Animal Farm, later relocated to New Hampshire. Many of the other houses on the farm were sold and converted into dwellings, some moved to other locations. Other buildings once used for farm purposes, such as the blacksmith shop, the hospital stable, the dog kennel, and so on, are today private homes. The long stable was cut into sections and sold to individuals who then moved them and made them into houses of their own. One need only look around the town and count the many houses that have the familiar Dutch Colonial shape to see Thomas W. Lawson's stamp. The enormous riding academy was dismantled and moved to the Brockton Fair Grounds, used as the agricultural hall until it was destroyed by fire in June 1933.

The Egypt gatehouse, used as the estate office, was purchased by Frank and Dolly Litchfield as a "fixer-upper," ready for occupancy in 1928. Dolly who served as secretary to Lawson from 1917 to 1925, saw the last days of the Copper King and helped arrange the removal of the famous silver dressing table to a private party in Hull, before the 1922 auction. The Litchfield's house contained many artifacts of the estate, including a silver horse-

Postscript

Below: Several artifacts can be found around town as well, such as this Dreamwold horse blanket chest, part of the Scituate Historical Society's permanent collection. (Photo by John J. Galluzzo) Right: With a quarter of a century having passed since their last paint job, the Scituate Historical Society began work on rebuilding the Dreamwold gates on Branch Street in 2000. (Photo by Glen Fields)

Beauty, Strength, Speed: Celebrating 100 Years of Thomas W. Lawson's Dreamwold

Left: Once restored, the gates will bring back memories of what once was one of the most talked about farms in American history. (Photo by Glen Fields) Right: Once the subject of near fistfights at Town Meeting, the Soldiers and Sailors Monument at Lawson Common stands its silent vigil. (Photo by John J. Galluzzo)

Postscript

The enormous riding academy building eventually burned to the ground. (Photo by T. E. Marr)

shoe from Lawson's famous racehorse Boralma, mounted in a prominent place, hung with the opening at the top, to insure good luck would not run out.

In 1982, Brookline architects Merrill H. Diamond and Gordon Hurwitz of Paren Corporation signed a purchase and sales agreement with the Ward's New Dreamwold Corporation, and later revealed plans for a condominium complex. The conversion would be in keeping with the architecture of Dreamwold Hall and would preserve its distinctive features. With town approval, the complex was completed in 1985.

On the evening of February 12, 1983, the people of Scituate held a "Romantic Farewell to Dreamwold" Benefit Dance. Judith Byrne Perry, general chairman, saw to the formation of committees and the solicitation of sponsors, representing almost every organization in town. Folks sipped cocktails and danced the hall into history to the strains of the Windjammer Band. An elaborate Closing Ceremony brought down the curtain on the greatest one-man show to ever hit town, as the residents of Scituate simply could not let Dreamwold close down without a fitting tribute to and remembrance of Tom Lawson.

Scituate's appreciation and enjoyment of the legacy of Tom Lawson extends to not only beautiful Lawson Common, but to the sensitive conversion of Dreamwold Hall and its environs. And finally, dominating the landscape, is the Tower, loved and admired as a signature of the town. Its bell chimes complete Lawson's legacy, sending a message of inspiration and continuity to everyone who hears them ring, a simple reminder that in America, anything is possible for anyone with a dream.

Postscript

Set in place with less fanfare, the World War I monument remains as impressively beautiful as it did when first designed. (Photo by John J. Galluzzo)

Wedding parties often stop to pose near the fountain on Lawson Common. (Photo by Sally Maish)

Postscript

Devastated by the loss of his wife Jeannie in 1906, Lawson collected white stones on the beaches of Scituate and lined the pathway to her final resting place. (Photo by T. E. Marr)

Beauty, Strength, Speed: Celebrating 100 Years of Thomas W. Lawson's Dreamwold

The simple Lawson memorial stones stand silently beneath a pair of cedar trees behind the Congregational Church on Country Way. (Photo by F. E. Gillis)

Select Bibliography

Newspapers
Boston Globe
Boston Traveler
Cohasset Sentinel
Hull Beacon
Quincy Patriot Ledger
Scituate Herald
Scituate Light
Scituate Mariner

Municipal Publications
Annual Report of the Officers of the Town of Scituate, 1900–1923.

Interviews
John Litchfield, interviewed by Carol Miles, February 3, 2002.
Mary Ward, interviewed by Carol Miles and John Galluzzo, January 29 and February 5, 2002.

Magazine Articles
Baldwin, Maurice. "The Country Estate of Thomas W. Lawson, Esq.," *The House Beautiful*, April 1903.

Lincoln, E. C. "Dreamwold: A Sportsman's Country Seat," *National Sportsman*, September 1902.

Robbins, Hayes. "An Old Town by the Sea," *New England Magazine*, 1902.

Lockley, Fred. "A Westerner at Thomas Lawson's Dreamwold," *Pacific Monthly Magazine*, December 1911.

———. "Along the South Shore," *Harper's New Monthly Magazine*, June 1878.

———. "'Dreamwold': The Farm of Thomas W. Lawson, Esq., Egypt, Mass.," *The Architectural Review*, September 1902.

Miscellaneous
Furlong, Charles Wellington. "Scituate: Past, Present and Future," an address read at the sixteenth anniversary of the Scituate Historical Society, September 10, 1932.

Lawson, Thomas W. "Dreamwold: The Farm of Thomas W. Lawson, Scituate, Massachusetts," a greeting to the members of the German Agricultural Society, June 23, 1903.

About the Authors

A love of books led Carol Miles to study first at Boston's Northeastern University part-time and then to obtain a B.A. from Goddard College in Vermont as part of their Adult Degree Program. She then went on to Simmons College, and, while working at the Massachusetts College of Pharmacy, she obtained her MSLIS in 1984. Along the way she married Paul Miles, whom she met while attending Potsdam State Teachers College in New York as a music major. They raised three children and are now the proud grandparents of five grandchildren. She has held several positions, including assistant archivist at the Scituate Town Archives and currently as archivist for the Scituate Historical Society.

A 1993 graduate of the University of Massachusetts at Amherst, John J. Galluzzo has pursued the study of history since finding inspiration at eleven years old on a Civil War battlefield in Kentucky. *Beauty, Strength, Speed* marks his fifth collaborative work on local history, the proceeds of which have all gone to local charities, while his sixth, *Then & Now: Scituate*, is due out in the summer of 2002. As executive director of the Scituate Historical Society, president of the Fort Revere Park & Preservation Society, and editor of the United States Life-Saving Service Heritage Association's *Wreck & Rescue Journal*, he has little spare time. Whatever time he does have he uses to improve the house and grounds of the Old Oaken Bucket Homestead in Scituate, where he currently lives.

Acknowledgments

The authors have numerous people to thank in connection with the "coming to life" of this book. No book of this scope on Tom Lawson could ever have been attempted without the work of the late Jane and "Chub" Chessia. They recognized early on that there was a tremendous story to be told about the Copper King's country estate, and collected photos, slides, magazine articles, news clippings, and whatever else they could find. Their slideshows delighted generations of Scituate residents. Today, their son Bob continues their work, actively researching the Lawson story, and this year for the first time delivering his own presentations, on behalf of the Scituate Historical Society, to the public.

Other researchers to whom we owe a debt of gratitude include David Corbin, who steered us toward a pile of dusty old scrapbooks when we were stuck looking for certain facts; Elise Walters and Mary Arcand, who have recently catalogued the Lawson photos in the possession of the Scituate Historical Society; and Barbara Maffucci and Betty Foster at the Town Archives who helped us locate specific Town Meeting articles relevant to the Tom Lawson story.

Several photographers have graciously allowed us to publish their images in this book, including Paul Miles, Glen Fields, Rudolph Mitchell, Charlotte Parsons, and Betty Miessner. Their images alone could make for a great book.

Of course, the entire project could never have been undertaken without the support and backing of the Trustees of the Scituate Historical Society; Fred Freitas, Peter Whitfield, Betty Miessner, Ruth Downton, Yvonne Twomey, Susan Phippen, and Duncan Bates Todd.

Any errors in this book fall squarely on the shoulders of the authors.

Today the United States abounds in magnificent estates and the beautiful homes of our wealthy families grace the hillsides and the vales of thousands of our towns and hamlets. It is not of the city houses that this article is to speak, but of the country residences, the gems of beauty tucked away in rural places far from noise and bustle, and the battle and strife of the busy world. Superior far to any city block, magnificent though it may be, these are the places which permit of a free scope for the artistic temperament, an unlimited chance for exercise of the love of the grand and the beautiful.

Our eastern states abound in these magnificent tributes to the taste, genius and refinement of America's men of wealth.

Massachusetts has its full share, and among them, preeminent in its perfection of loveliness, one shines forth supreme.

It is of the latest conspicuous creation of this class that this article is to speak in particular. It is of Dreamwold . . . an enchanted fairyland, the creation of a man's genius, pluck, and indomitable persistence. He took a piece of bleakest New England, a barren and sterile territory, covered with stones and rocks. This he transformed into a paradise.

—E. C. Lincoln, in *The National Sportsman*